The English Highwayman

The English Highwayman

A Legend Unmasked

PETER HAINING

ROBERT HALE · LONDON

First published in Great Britain 1991

ISBN 0 7090 4426 7

Robert Hale Limited
Clerkenwell House
Clerkenwell Green
London EC1R 0HT

Photoset in Ehrhardt by
Derek Doyle & Associates.
Printed in Great Britain by
St Edmundsbury Press, Bury St Edmunds, Suffolk.
Bound by WBC Bookbinders Ltd, Bridgend, Glamorgan.

Contents

Acknowledgements

A number of people were generous with their time and help in the writing of this book and I should particularly like to thank that indefatigable researcher W.O.G. Lofts who unearthed a number of the best stories told herein, as well as James Hinton, Paul Fitzgerald, Colin Matthews, Alan Sanders, Linda Doxey, Jane Byrne and the members of staff of the London Library, British Museum and British Newspaper Library who all provided invaluable assistance. I am grateful, too, to the following organizations for their permission to include copyright material: British Film Institute, The Cannon Group, *The Times, Illustrated London News, Country Life, Evening Standard, York Evening News, East Anglian Monthly, Radio Times, Sunday Mirror* and the *Daily Mail.* A special thank you also to my editor, Rachel Wright, for her care and attention to the manuscript.

List of Illustrations

Between pages 80 and 81

Between pages 128 and 129

1 The Highwaymen: Freebooters or Felons?

Until a few years ago, a man who looked uncannily like the popular conception of Dick Turpin lived in a little eighteenth-century cottage in a village just outside York. He was a short, stockily built fellow known as Nick Blackmore and he had a mania for highwaymen.

Nick collected everything and anything pertaining to the history of the 'Gentlemen of the Road'; in particular, items related to Turpin and his period. To enter his home was, in fact, rather like stepping back into history, for every wall in the place was hung with old pistols, swords, muskets, wanted posters and prints of many of England's most famous highwaymen. It was said – not without good reason – that his collection was the envy of every museum curator who knew of its existence.

Nick's mania even extended to dressing like his heroes: wearing white ruffled shirts, long-tailed coats, breeches, buckled shoes and a three-cornered highwayman's hat. He smoked long, white clay pipes, drank from pewter mugs and ate his meals from wooden platters. He also addressed his visitors in the courteous tones of an eighteenth-century gentleman. 'Good-day, sir,' he would answer any knock at his door, 'and pray what can I do for you?'

His only companion in the house was his aged mother, a tiny, silent old lady who wore a woollen, ankle-length dress and a large white bonnet that made her look like one of the Pilgrim Fathers' womenfolk. No other living creature shared Nick's life, though in the living-room stood a huge rocking-horse called 'Black Bess' which he rode furiously for half an hour every day to give himself exercise and work up an appetite.

He was said to be an expert swordsman and, on more than one occasion, had taken down the most deadly of his weapons to see off intruders who had ill-advisedly broken into the cottage assuming him to be a harmless old eccentric. And when he had been told by one visitor, to whom he had demonstrated another of his razor-sharp implements, that he ought perhaps to keep a rubber tip on the point, he had replied, 'Bah, my good sir – what's a drop of blood? Fencers today are all soft, those of King George's day were far superior!'

Nick Blackmore was also an unimpeachable expert on the history of highway robbery in England. His library was lined with old volumes of criminal history, alongside bound collections of the pamphlets and broadsheets which used to be published in the immediate aftermath of the execution of a highwayman. He had many novels, too, the glamorized lives of Dick Turpin, Claude Duval, Jonathan Wild and others like them; as well as innumerable files of yellowing cuttings, all relating to the one subject.

A visit to Nick Blackmore's cottage must have been, truly, an unforgettable experience. The twentieth century seemed to have been quite unable to intrude into it anywhere: there was no running water, no electricity, certainly no radio, television or phone. Water had to be drawn from the well in the garden; candles illuminated the low-beamed rooms; and all the meals were cooked on an open hearth that had not changed since the cottage was built. There was not even a front doorbell, only a large iron knocker.

Inside this retreat, Nick would sit by the wood fire, a pint of mead in one hand and a clay pipe in the other, and recount the history of the highwaymen almost as if he had lived it. In truth, he *did* live it day by day, anxious to keep alive the legend of what he believed to have been the most exciting and colourful period of history.

When old Mrs Blackmore and Nick died within a year of each other, there were fears amongst his small circle of friends that the collection might be dispersed and, with it, an absolutely unique source of highway history. In fact, Nick had already made provision for this eventuality and a solicitor in York saw to the careful disposal of all the material to the various museum collections where it would be most appreciated.

Today, the result of Nick Blackmore's years of painstaking research and endeavour are to be found enriching several of the best collections of information about the period. Although I never had the opportunity to meet Nick, I know this to be true because I have consulted material that was once in his library. And though Blackmore was not his real name – which I have been specifically asked not to divulge – his memory lives on in these pages, for he is just one more example of humankind's enduring interest in the history of the English highwayman … and woman.

It is said that Nick often worried that interest in highwaymen was declining. Yet if he had only taken a newspaper occasionally, listened to the radio sometimes, watched television or seen a film, even broken his most firmly held rule not to travel by car or train, he would have been aware of an increasing public fascination with the 'Knights of the Road'.

He would have read, for instance, how a rise in petrol prices was headlined by the *Daily Mail* in September 1990 with the highwayman's traditional cry of 'Stand and Deliver!'; while on the fashion page of the *Guardian* a month later, women readers were being encouraged to wear 'a very dashing full-length highwayman coat with a huge cape collar'. He might also have noticed an advertisement by Royal Doulton for a new, limited edition figurine of Dick Turpin, the 'most notorious and wanted highwayman', being produced in a limited edition to 'commemorate the 250th anniversary of his capture and execution'.

If Nick had ever watched television he might have seen repeats of the series *Dick Turpin* starring Richard O'Sullivan. Had he even been in a cinema, he might have viewed one of the many film versions of the story ranging from the first silent movie, *Dick Turpin's Ride to York* (1922) with Matheson Lang, to the various American 'adaptations' starring Tom Mix (1925), Victor McLaglen (1933), Louis Hayward (1951) and David Weston (1965). He could have enjoyed Columbia Pictures' recreation of the famous Alfred Noyes poem in *The Highwayman* (1951), and the two adaptations of the story of the notorious highwaywoman, Lady Catherine Ferrers, entitled *The Wicked Lady* and featuring, respectively, Margaret Lockwood and Faye Dunaway.

Other examples would have caught his eye, too: the public houses cashing in on their associations with famous highwaymen; the restoration of several lock-ups and old buildings which once housed these men; and, of course, a number of roads in and around London that bear names forever associated with the best-known members of the fraternity. The examples, like the legend itself, just go on ...

It has been claimed that the difference between a highwayman and a footpad was simply: a horse. Though this is to a degree true, it is far too simplistic an explanation. For in the criminal hierarchy this meant the difference between officers and other ranks. Highwaymen were the aristocrats of robbers, it was said, and they aroused much romantic interest. Not a few were renowned for their courtesy and chivalry on the road.

Indeed, it was not just anyone who could climb on to the back of a horse and become a successful highwayman, as Lord Macaulay argued in his monumental *History of England* (1861):

> It was necessary to the success and even to the safety of the highwayman that he should be a bold and skilful rider, and that his manners and appearance should be such as suited the master of a fine horse. He therefore held an aristocratical position in the community of thieves, appeared at fashionable coffee houses and gaming houses, and betted with men of quality on the race ground. Sometimes, indeed, he was a man of good family and education.
>
> A romantic interest therefore attached, and perhaps still attaches, to the names of the freebooters of this class. The vulgar eagerly drank in tales of their ferocity and audacity, of their occasional acts of generosity and good nature, of their amours, of their miraculous escapes, of their desperate struggles, and of their manly bearing at the bar and in the cart.

There were, however, exceptions to this rule – quite a number of them. There were always cruel and vicious felons who sometimes killed their victims after robbing them; who would not think twice about betraying their friends of either sex; and who went screaming and begging for mercy to their well-deserved executions. As Gordon S. Maxwell has written in his *Gangsters' London* (1938):

> These 'Gentlemen of the Road' were no more respecters of places than they were of persons, and the streets of London were often as dangerous as the wilds of Hounslow Heath or Epping Forest. Places we now look upon as civilised and safe were then, as likely as not, the lurking places of desperate highwaymen

> ready to pounce upon the unsuspecting wayfarer who, relieved of his valuables, watched his attacker disappear into one of the copses or alleys beside every highway. The chronicles of crime contain innumerable cases of this sort, especially during the seventeenth century and through the eighteenth, when highwaymen were part and parcel of everyday life.

Although the history of the English highwayman only covers about two hundred years, from the early 1600s to just into the 1800s, the origins of the 'profession' go back far beyond that time. Interestingly, the very word 'highwayman' was originally three words, with the emphasis being on the word 'way'. An example of this is to be found in the Thomasson Tracts of 1549, lodged in the British Museum, which declare: 'This last session there suffered 28, most of them high way men.'

If there is, though, one man whom historians believe was the original English highwayman, then it has to be the most famous figure of the Middle Ages: Robin Hood.

Of course, researchers into the life of the 'Outlaw of Sherwood Forest' soon discover exactly the same problems as those faced by anyone writing about highwaymen: the evidence is quite often contradictory and much of the source material was compiled by people seeking to justify whatever social or moral viewpoint they were pursuing. The modern writer just has to plough through as much of the original documentation as still exists and examine and sift it carefully.

There have been those historians who are convinced that Robin never existed at all: that his deeds were actually those of a Frenchman adopted by English legend. Others have claimed that he lived sometime around the thirteenth century; could well have been the grandson of Ralph Fitzooth (a companion of William the Conqueror); and, when he fell upon hard times, was forced to make a living from the countryside by his skill as an archer.

What seems much more open to debate is that the outlaw and his band of followers confined themselves solely to Sherwood Forest. Just as the highwayman often needed to shift his locality to avoid capture, so Robin is believed to have moved across a number of counties including Nottinghamshire, Yorkshire, Derbyshire and Lincolnshire, where place names still exist today to record his presence.

One fact beyond dispute is that he is first mentioned in print in the English poet William Langland's epic, *Vision of William concerning Piers the Plowman*, written in about 1362, in which he is referred to as 'Robin Hode'. It was well over a century later before the first full account of his adventures was published by Wynkyn de Worde in *A Lytel Geste of Robyn Hoode*, which appeared in 1495.

Later chroniclers went on to develop the now-familiar portrait of Robin as an outlaw on horseback who robbed the rich to help the poor and was assisted by a band of equally resolute friends. His bravery and ability to outwit the arrogant barons who pursued him, plus his skill as a rider and swordsman, made him a hero of the people. The legend was further enhanced because Robin was believed to have been handsome and strong, a good lover and a faithful friend, not to mention having a fine sense of humour. Two hundred years later, these qualities were to be seen as the hallmark of the best highwaymen.

Some historians have argued that the legend of Robin Hood was one of the factors that sustained the poor and oppressed of England through those next two centuries as they, like their predecessors, looked for a hero to challenge again those set in brutal authority over them. The highwayman, when he appeared, had some of Robin Hood's qualities, and this has been advanced as an explanation for the popularity the men of the road enjoyed during their heyday as well as the fascination they have exerted ever since. As one writer, Joseph Gollomb, subscribing to this argument said some years back, Robin Hood was not only the father of highwaymen, he was also their patron saint.

Of course, travellers had been robbed while on their journeys across England for centuries, but the highwaymen were also something of a by-product of the invention of the flintlock pistol late in the seventeenth century, and the growth of traffic on the main roads leading out of London. As the towns across the country grew bigger and richer and the need for travel by merchants or wealthy pleasure-seekers developed apace, so the opportunities for robbers multiplied.

The era also saw important developments in the methods of transportation. At first there were just the clumsy, horse-drawn coaches, with their iron wheels and lack of springing, which lurched and swayed painfully over the hard summer roads and wallowed in the winter mud. Then, in their place, came the properly sprung and much lighter and faster two- and four-wheeled coaches. These vehicles, apart from carrying four passengers inside – and perhaps the same number outside – were also used later for transporting the mail, an even bigger temptation to those with their eyes on the main chance.

But there were still plenty of people who preferred to travel on horseback – after all, a single horse moved a lot faster than a coach, at about five m.p.h., and a carriage's interior could be crowded and uncomfortable, too. Such lone riders were by far the most popular victims of the highwaymen, and it was only the more daring robbers who would take on a coach which, though the potential booty was better, might also contain armed citizenry.

The greatest advantage of all for the highwaymen, however, was that, until well into the second half of the eighteenth century, there was no effective police-force in England whatsoever. There were unpaid parish constables and nightwatchmen, to be sure, and highway robbery was a capital offence, but none of these proved a deterrent to the mounted robbers.

It is one of the curious features of the history of the highwaymen that although they risked being hanged for the very act of carrying out a hold-up – as a capital offence, it mattered not in the least to the law whether it was done chivalrously or with the most terrible bloodshed – only a small percentage of them committed murder as well. This seems against all logic at a time when life was considered cheap, and the fact has created a lasting puzzle for criminologists. For killing the victim would have had two distinct advantages: delaying pursuit and eliminating the only witness to the crime. It was the great eighteenth-century savant Dr Samuel Johnson who argued, 'To equal robbery with murder is to reduce murder to robbery – if only murder was punished with death, very few robbers would stain their hands in blood.'

But the indisputable fact remains that few highwaymen killed their victims. Records from the time clearly show that eighteenth-century England had by far the most robbers and yet the lowest murder rate in Europe.

Two locations will be seen to feature in the lives of almost every highwayman who was brought to book: Newgate and

Tyburn. Both names brought a shiver to the spine of any man, or woman, who chose highway robbery as their career: for there was very little chance of escape from the first and none at all from the second.

Newgate, which is celebrated in the famous collection of accounts of its most notorious inmates, the *Newgate Calendar* (first published in 1774, extensively revised in 1826, and frequently published ever since), was a prison for the criminals of London and Middlesex. Originally one of the seven gates of London, it was established in the twelfth century, rebuilt after the Great Fire, and again in 1780, and finally demolished in 1903. The site is now occupied by the Central Criminal Court, the famous Old Bailey.

It was to Newgate that arrested highwaymen were brought to await trial. Here the types of cells in which they lived were entirely dependent on their means. Those who had nothing suffered the most appalling conditions; while those who could pay for their keep enjoyed clean, airy rooms where they could – and frequently did – entertain their relatives and friends until they had been tried and, inevitably, found guilty and condemned to death.

There seems little doubt that many highwaymen confessed readily to their crimes, their vanity unable to contain their tongues. The notoriety to which this gave rise inevitably brought large numbers of curious citizens to visit them – on payment of an 'admission fee' to the governor and gaolers, of course! Those of their number who had lived ostentatiously often died the same way, with women of all ranks who had been their lovers and mistresses clamouring for a tearful farewell.

Tyburn, three miles from Newgate, was the place where the highwayman went to meet his maker – and his public. The more famous the robber, the bigger the crowd that would see him on his way, and the higher the standard of behaviour he would be expected to observe as he was executed. The 'Tyburn Tree' was actually the popular name for the Middlesex gallows which stood close to that famous modern London landmark, the Marble Arch. The first hanging was apparently held there in 1196.

The gallows consisted of a permanent structure of three uprights, joined at the top by three beams forming an equilateral triangle. This was known by analogy as the 'triple tree' or 'the gallows tree'. For many years, the last solid place beneath a hanged man's feet had been the rung of a ladder, and it was the hangman's job to give this a sudden, sharp twist so that the condemned might be said to have been 'turned off', to use a commonly heard expression. During the era of the highwaymen, however, most prisoners were driven to Tyburn in carts which were placed under the beams and, when the noose was in place, driven away smartly. As death might not always be instantaneous, a prisoner who did not wish to risk undue suffering would tip the hangman to see the operation was performed correctly, or, should he not die quickly, to have the man pull on his legs to hasten the end.

The body of a prisoner had to remain hanging for at least half an hour, after which it was cut down and the clothes removed by the hangman as his perquisite. If the highwayman had friends or relatives they could then claim the corpse for burial; if not, he would most likely end up in the hands of the surgeons for public anatomizing. The bodies of some of the more notorious felons were wrapped in tarred canvas and hung in chains (actually strips of metal bands) from roadside gibbets at the scene of their crimes, as a lesson to other malefactors.

Hangings at Tyburn were said to be among London's most popular public spectacles, and, in addition to thousands of people lining the streets, wealthier men and women would hire seats in the specially built stands, while aristocrats watched from balconies overlooking the scene as they enjoyed a champagne breakfast. Any prisoner who failed to dress well, conduct himself with spirit, or die with dignity, could expect to be heartily booed and even showered with rubbish. In the eighteenth century, when highwaymen were at their most numerous across the country, whole cartloads of prisoners would be driven from Newgate every six weeks for what became ghoulishly known as 'Tyburn Fair'.

The men of the road who ended their careers in this way were a mixed and varied breed, as the reader will discover in the chapters which follow. Some, it seems, were freebooters, exemplified in the dying speech of one of their number, Isaac Atkinson, the son of a Berkshire squire, who told the crowd around Tyburn, 'Gentlemen, there's nothing like a merry life, and a short one.' Others were little more than common felons who themselves lived in fear, in turn using it as the prime weapon against their victims. Some highwaymen always worked alone, others in pairs, a number in gangs. The proceeds they might expect could range from a few pence from a poor clergyman to thousands of pounds in money and valuables from the rich and powerful.

The constants in the life of most highwaymen seem to have been their black mask and long cloak, their standard command to 'Stand and deliver!' and the doxy all the men kept as lover and accomplice. For much of the period in which they flourished, they had favourite haunts on the main roads out of London. The Great North Road was a magnet for many of the most famous, as were Finchley Common, Hounslow Heath, Shotover Hill on the Oxford Road, and Shooters Hill at Woolwich.

In recounting the rise and fall of the English highwayman, I have tried to unmask some of the real facts about these extraordinary men and women. Some, like Dick Turpin, for instance, were not at all the romantic figures that many accounts would have us believe; while others, such as Captain Zachary Howard (the Cavalier who robbed Oliver Cromwell) and John 'Swift Nicks' Nevison (the man who *really* rode to York) have never been given the full credit to which they are entitled.

Although we shall doubtless never know all the facts about these gentlemen – and women – of the road, it is satisfying at least to be able to dispel some of the myths and re-establish a few of the reputations. And few are perhaps more deserving of this than Moll Cutpurse who has every right to claim the title of 'The Mother of Highwaymen' …

2 The First Highwayman Was a Woman

In the early years of the seventeenth century a familiar sight on the streets of Holborn and Fleet Street was a flamboyant figure known as Moll Cutpurse, who dressed in men's clothing and invariably had a tobacco-pipe stuck rakishly in her mouth. As outlandish in her way as a modern punk, Moll turned many heads as she strode about the locality dressed in a pointed hat covering her dark, curly locks, a black cloak over a colourful doublet and hose, and with a sword hanging by her side. Tall of stature, with challenging blue eyes, she appealed as strongly, sexually, to women as to men, and rejoiced in the nickname public acclaim had given her, the 'Roaring Girl'.

Moll Cutpurse was also, the evidence suggests, the very first highwayman – not to mention 'The Mother of Highwaywomen', to quote the social historian Patrick Pringle. Though rumour and legend have done much to elaborate or alter many of the facts of this unique woman's life, research does lead to the conclusion that she highlighted her career of crime by appearing as a robber on the roads of London and was, at the very least, a contemporary of the first highwaymen if not their actual predecessor. Records also indicate that she claimed for herself the accolade of being the first female smoker!

Moll certainly possessed the capability to be a successful highwaywoman. She was a skilful horsewoman, knew the highways and byways of London and its suburbs intimately, and was a fine shot with a pistol. From childhood she had also developed a talent second to none at relieving the gentry of London of any valuables they might carry about their persons. Even when challenged by someone in authority it was said she spoke with the commanding tone of a general – although she was also perfectly capable of swearing like a trooper!

Small wonder, then, that a contemporary account says of her:

'There's a wench called Moll, mad Moll or Merry Moll – a creature so strange in quality a whole city takes note of her name and person!' (Interestingly, among those who 'took note of her' was a playwright named Shakespeare, who alluded to her in his play *Twelfth Night*, through Sir Toby Belch's reference to things being hid 'like Mistress Mall's picture'.)

Re-examining today the contemporary documents and accounts of the life of Moll Cutpurse produces a number of interesting facts which many of the later versions have avoided or glossed over – the writers probably being restrained from using the information by the moral attitudes of their times.

Some early sources, for instance, declare that Moll's neighbours believed she was a hermaphrodite – and even when the contrary was reported after her death, the belief nevertheless persisted in both story and ballad. In fact, she was bisexual, as happy to go to bed with women as men, and is quoted on this very subject by the Jacobean playwright Thomas Middleton, who with Thomas Dekker created a highly successful play, *The Roaring Girl* while the subject was still very much alive:

'I have no humour to marry,' Moll told the writer, 'for I love to lie a' both sides a' th' bed ... I have the head of myself and am man enough for any woman.'

Her fondness for men's clothing should not, though, be seen as just an element of her sexual proclivities: disguise undoubtedly helped her in her criminal exploits, and by employing more than the simple face mask (which became the traditional sign of the highwayman), she used a full change into a dress to throw pursuers off her trail. It seems highly likely, too, that by impersonating a man, she ensured that many of her crimes were mistakenly ascribed to others, thereby making it impossible now, unfortunately, to estimate the number of robberies she actually committed.

Some authorities have stated that Moll was an ugly woman, dirty and mean-spirited, and more interested in masculine than feminine pursuits. This, however, hardly coincides with Middleton's description of her as a 'handsome and graceful woman', kind-hearted and generous in her dealings with other criminals; a woman who covered the walls of her house with looking-glasses and amused herself with lovers of both sexes – many of whom were seemingly unaware of her double life. This merely seems to me to confirm her mastery of disguise and deception!

Another claim, that she was really no more than a common pickpocket – hence her name – and only prospered through trading in the ill-gotten gains of other highway robbers – is also refuted by the first biographer of highwaymen, Captain Alexander Smith, who wrote in his now rare work, *A Complete History of the Most Notorious Highwayman* (1719), completed less than a hundred years after the event:

> A long time had Moll Cutpurse robbed on the road, but at last robbing General Fairfax of 250 Jacobuses [Gold coins struck during the reign of James I and variously worth between 50 and 125 pence] on Hounslow Heath, whom she shot through the arm in opposing her, a close pursuit was made after her by some Parliamentarian officers. Her horse failing her at Turnham Green they there apprehended her and carried her to Newgate, after which she was condemned; but she procured her pardon by giving her adversary £2,000. Now Moll being frightened by this disaster, she left off going on the highway any more and took a house within two doors of the Globe Tavern in Fleet Street where she turned fence, a buyer of stolen goods, by which occupation she got a great deal of money. Her reputation soon grew, the more so when tobacco became a great mode and she being mightily taken with the pastime of smoking, because of its singularity and that no woman ever smoked before her, though a great many of the sex since have followed her example.

Even in this terse account, it is not difficult to appreciate that Moll Cutpurse was obviously an extraordinary woman whose influence on the legend of the English highwayman is both important and enduring, and deserves further investigation. All the more so, I believe, in the light of another comment by a respected historian, Christopher Hibbert, who wrote recently, in *Highwaymen* (1967) ‘As a highwaywoman she seems, indeed, to have been more successful than any of her eighteenth century male successors’.

The first interesting fact to be gleaned about Moll Cutpurse is that this was not her real name at all. She was born Mary Frith in the year 1584, the daughter of a shoemaker who carried out his trade in Aldersgate Street, in the Barbican district of London. According to a little booklet, *The Life and Death of Mrs. Mary Frith, Commonly Called Mal Cutpurse*, published in 1662 ‘for the Delight and Recreation of all Merry Disposed Persons’, the child grew up as a 'very tomrig and rumpscuttle' – in other words, a tomboy. The anonymous work also reports that Mary was born with her fists tightly clenched, 'a sure sign of a wild and adventurous nature'.

Mary was an only child, and, despite her unruly disposition, was spoiled and indulged by her doting parents. She was given a good education and taught to ride, but soon found the pursuits of the opposite sex more interesting than her own and began falling into bad company. Before she had entered her teens she was frequenting bear-baitings and wrestling matches and proving more than a match for any young man who challenged her right to be in such places. 'She worsted many a pretty fellow in fair fight with a quarterstaff', according to the above account.

Mr Frith's original plan to put his rebellious daughter into domestic service was abandoned as her exploits about London grew wilder, and for a time he thought of agreeing to her demands to have 'a man's job' by apprenticing her to a saddler. Instead, though, he listened to the advice of his brother, a minister of the church, who maintained that the only cure for the troublesome girl would be to pack her off to America to work on a plantation! Mary was, in fact, actually put on board a merchant ship at Gravesend bound for New England, but somehow managed to jump overboard before the vessel sailed and swim to shore. From this moment, she was a free spirit determined to follow her own nature and inclinations.

Back in London, Mary naturally enough fell into a life of crime to support herself, and, by the turn of the century, had become 'distinguished in the different characters of bully, prostitute, procuress, fortune-teller, thief, pickpocket, and receiver of stolen goods', to quote *The Life and Death*. Because of the generally accepted role of women at this time as servant or mother, Mary's deliberate decision to wear male clothing to enhance the impact of her height, as well as her robust language earned her her sobriquet, 'roaring', which was a less-than-flattering adjective for a woman of the era.

Quite when this 'lusty and sturdy wench', as Captain Alexander Smith called her, first took to robbing travellers on the highway is difficult to establish precisely; but certainly she had a reputation as a skilled thief and pick-pocket by the time she was fifteen, and was working in company with a gang who frequented the bear garden in Southwark. Her accomplices were not, it seems, altogether trustworthy, for male envy at her exploits soon lead to whispers about her crimes reaching the authorities. A series of arrests followed which enraged Mary, now becoming widely known as 'Moll Cutpurse', and she decided that a solitary career in crime might carry fewer risks. Captain Smith has again recorded the relevant facts:

> But having been very often in Old Bridewell, the Compters and Newgate for her irregular practices, and burned in the hand four times, Moll left off this petty sort of theft and went on the highway, committing many great robberies, but all of them on the Roundheads or rebels that fomented the Civil War against Charles I.

Moll, with her skill as a rider, her ability to handle firearms, plus her mastery of disguise, was well-enough armed to confront and rob those foolish enough to travel the roads about London without protection. Early in her career, she found that the best pickings were to be had in the vicinity of Hounslow Heath, which was later to become such a popular spot with other highwaymen.

It was, though, to be some years before these audacious robberies were ascribed to Moll, as all her victims swore they had been taken by a man. And, doubtless, even those who suspected the sex of the person behind the pistols were reluctant to say so for fear of ridicule at being robbed by a woman!

What undoubtedly cemented the fame of Moll Cutpurse was the play by Middleton and Dekker, *The Roaring Girl*, which was first performed in 1611 at the Fortune Theatre, and proved a huge success. The two dramatists had judged well the public interest in this larger-than-life figure in men's clothes who always seemed one step ahead of the law. Indeed, no member of the audience was left in any doubt that the 'heroine' was the self-same Moll who was currently reigning as the queen of the London underworld.

'She's the spirit of four great parishes', one character in the play declares, 'and a voice that will drown all the city. Methinks a brave captain might get all his soldiers upon her and never hold her.'

Another agrees with this verdict: ' 'Tis the maddest

fantasticalest girl! I never knew so much flesh and so much nimbleness put together.'

What makes this play so valuable in any study of Moll Cutpurse's life is not just the fact that Middleton and Dekker were writing about a contemporary person, but that Dekker had, like Middleton, met the woman and caroused with her in the Fleet Street taverns which she haunted. The words which he puts in her mouth ring with the sound of authenticity.

'I know more laws', she declares at one point as she slips into the slang language, or cant, of the London underworld:

> Of cheaters, lifters, nips, foists, puggards, curbers,
> With all the devil's black-guard, than it's fit,
> Should be discover'd to a noble wit.
> I know they have their orders, offices,
> Circuits, and circles, unto which they're bound,
> To raise their own damnation in.

And, proud of her own reputation, Moll adds:

> Condemn me? Troth, and you should, sir,
> I'd make you seek out one to hang in my place:
> I'd give you the slip at the gallows and cozen the people!

Not everyone admired Moll Cutpurse, however, for there were those who objected to the way she cocked a snook at the law and affronted decent society by dressing in men's clothes. Indeed, action was taken after she had ridden across London from Charing Cross to Shoreditch in a particularly outlandish set of clothes, waving a banner and blowing a trumpet, to win a twenty-pound bet. For this she was arrested. The 1662 pamphlet 'quotes' the lady herself on this incident:

> Some promoting Apparitor, set on by an adversary of mine, whom I could never punctually know, cited me to appear in the Court of the Arches, where was an Accusation exhibited against me for wearing indecent and manly apparel. I was advised by my Proctor to demur to the Jurisdiction of the Court, as for a Crime, if such, not cognizable there or elsewhere; but he did it to spin out my Cause, and get my Money; for in the conclusion I was sentenced there to stand and do Penance in a White Sheet at Paul's Cross, during morning Sermon on a Sunday.

Swallowing her anger at this deception, Moll performed her

sentence – though another report claims that the tears she shed were those of a 'maudlin drunk, it being discovered she had tipple'd of three quarts of sack (six pints) before she came to her penance'. Within hours, however, bold as ever, she was back on the streets of Holborn in full male regalia and ready to continue her career of crime.

Records indicate that Moll's most famous act of highway robbery was the attack on Oliver Cromwell's man, General Fairfax, on Hounslow Heath, which ended disastrously when her horse went lame at Turnham Green and she was captured. Yet she had the money to buy her freedom – any prisoner who had not committed treason or murder could secure their release for a minimum of £500, popular legend had it – and thereafter she settled for a quiet life in a house in Fleet Street, almost opposite Shoe Lane and Salisbury Court. Here she became far-famed as the best fence (receiver of stolen goods) in London: so well known, in fact, that those who lost property to the depredations of pick-pockets or highwaymen soon took to visiting Moll's establishment, for there was every chance of their valuables turning up there and being readily redeemable for a consideration. As Charles G. Harper has explained in his important work, *Half-Hours With The Highwaymen* (1908):

> In those halcyon days of the receivers of stolen property, before the evil career of Jonathan Wild had caused an Act of Parliament to be passed, dealing with them on the same footing as the actual thieves, much was done in the way of ransom and ready brokerage, and, so long as it was done with discretion, with advantage to all concerned. The owners got their own again, with the expenditure of a comparatively trifling sum, the gang carried on their operations with a large degree of security, and the wily Moll made an excellent income. She was witty and original, and – such was the spirit of the age – she became rather the fashion among the riotous young blades of town, who were then 'seeing life'. The highwaymen knew her well, and resorted to her house when they had taken watches and jewellery they could not themselves, without the gravest risk, endeavour to sell. They trusted her, and the public, coming to redeem the articles, did the same; and indeed, as intermediary between losers and finders, she was honesty itself: absolutely beyond suspicion.'

An interesting rumour that developed about Moll at this time – which she did nothing to dispel – suggested that her success at being able to recover stolen property was due to the fact that she owned a pair of magic glasses which enabled her to 'see' where the missing valuables were and institute their immediate recovery with the aid of her associates!

Captain Alexander Smith has also explained how Moll pursued her sexual inclinations. He writes:

> In order to get money she would stick out to bawd for either men or women, insomuch that her house became a double temple for Priapus and Venus, frequented by votaries of both sorts; who, being generous to her labour, their desires were favourably accommodated with expedition, while she lingered with others, delaying their impatience by laying before them the difficult but certain attainment of their wishes. This served as a spur to the dullness of their purses, for the lady Pecunia and she kept the same pace; but still in the end she did the feat.

It seems likely that Moll provided refuge for a number of highwaymen when the authorities were close on their trail. As an ardent Royalist, she had little time for Cromwell's men and during the years of the Commonwealth she happily encouraged those who wished to persecute or rob the hated oppressors.

Indeed, it is true to say that Moll Cutpurse's dearest wish was to live long enough to see the restoration of the monarchy, and although her last years were spent in the comfort provided by her trade in stolen property, she finally died of the unromantic disease of dropsy at the fine old age of seventy-five on 26 July 1659 – just one year before the return of Charles II. She was buried in St Bride's churchyard, appropriately in one of the suits of men's clothing that she had worn during her life. Somewhat surprisingly, though, considering all the money she had made as a highwaywoman and fence, Moll left just £100 – of which twenty pounds, she declared in her will, was to be kept for her friends and associates to drink the health of the king when he was once again on the throne.

With the passing of the 'Roaring Girl', highway robbery may have lost its 'mother', but the 'sons' she left behind were already cutting a swath of robbery – around the outskirts of London and across parts of the English countryside – that history would never forget.

Few of Moll's associates, however, were the equal of a certain

Captain James Hind, a bold and dashing highwayman who became known as 'The Grand Thief of England'. He had been a friend of Moll's for years, and raised a glass and smoked a pipe with her on a number of occasions. His exploits had made him a household name and had gained him the admiration of many members of the female population.

It is the remarkable Captain Hind, who has been rightly described as the first important English highwayman, who now occupies centre stage in the next part of our colourful story ...

3 'The Grand Thief of England'

If any one man can be said to have been the archetypal highwayman as popular legend would have him – a dashing figure on horseback who robbed coaches with a flourish of his pistol and a doff of his hat – it was certainly Captain James Hind, who, like Moll Cutpurse, was celebrated in broadsheets, booklets and a stage play.

Hind, with his flowing hair and piercing eyes, his courage and resourcefulness, displayed chivalry to ladies, courtesy to male victims, and took a leaf from the 'Robin Hood' tradition by sometimes returning to the poor what he had taken from the rich. Some accounts of the captain make him seem more like a Casanova of the road than a highwayman – for he also pursued the opposite sex with single-minded determination and, amongst his various lovers, gossip listed the youngest daughter of a duke.

In fact, the captain's legend grew first in popular rumour and newspaper reports, then in sensational pamphlets and books such as *The English Gusman*, and finally, in a play curiously entitled, *The Prince of Prigs* (1651) which claimed to reveal: 'The practices of that grand Thief Captain James Hind, relating Divers of his Pranks and Exploits, never heretofore published by any.' By combining all of these sources it is possible to reconstruct a fairly accurate picture of the life and career of the first major highwayman.

James Hind was born the son of a saddler in 1616 at Chipping Norton in Oxfordshire. An only child, he was doted upon by his mother but, while still at school, revealed a restless nature, and at the age of fifteen was apprenticed to a local butcher. It has been alleged that the butcher treated young Hind badly – certainly he served less than two years at the trade before running away – but freed of this tyranny he managed to secure a 'loan' of three pounds from his mother and decided to seek his fortune in London.

Although Hind was still only in his middle teens, 'he soon contracted a relish for the pleasures of the town', according to one of his chapbook biographies; 'and a bottle and a female companion became his principal delight and occupied the greater part of his time'.

Despite the young man's resourceful charm, his money did not last long and he saw crime as the way of answering his need for more. He may, indeed, have committed a number of thefts before he became involved in a drunken riot in a Fleet Street tavern and was thrown into the local lock-up, known as the Poultry Compter. Here, when he awoke the following morning amidst the evil-smelling criminal fraternity, he came face to face with one Thomas Allen, 'an expert in most thievish arts', who was profoundly to influence the course of his future.

Whether the cunning and unscrupulous Allen just took a liking to Hind – or more probably sensed a young man who would be of use to him – the two later left the Compter as friends. Allen was the leader of a gang of thieves and introduced Hind to the others, who insisted the young man demonstrate his dedication to the criminal arts before he could be admitted to their ranks. The task they set the teenager was to rob a traveller on Shooters Hill, the famous road in South London. Allen and the others would conceal themselves nearby, they said, but would only interfere if the hold-up went wrong. A contemporary account relates what happened next.

> At Shooters Hill, meeting with a gentleman and his servant, Hind had the courage to rob them of £15 without the assistance of his companions. However, our new highwayman was so generous as to give the gentleman back twenty shillings of his money, 'for handsel's sake' he declared to the startled soul, to bear his charges on his journey.

The hold-up left Allen and the other watching men filled with a mixture of admiration and surprise. The boy had certainly acquitted himself with all the panache of a veteran – but *why* return some of the money? Hind explained with a grin that a 'handsel' was a present given on a special occasion to ensure good luck in the future. He could, though, have had little idea at that moment that the gesture would not only bring him luck in his future career but also establish the pattern of his operations – as well as being imitated by other highwaymen. Charles Harper explains:

> Here was an intrepid youngster, the coolest hand at robbery, courteously giving back a percentage of his honest (*sic*) earnings. They were witnessing the foundation of a new school in an old art, a school that, although its fit pupils were few and far between, did at least establish a tradition that, while it did not greatly advantage the travelling world, did at least serve to win a long line of highwaymen an amount of forbearance that seems to us moderns almost incredible. The law visited highway robbery with sentences of the utmost ferocity, but individuals, as a general rule, took their losses, not only with astonishing philosophy, but with a remarkable display of good nature. Hind was not yet the holder of a commission, but he was evidently already captain of himself.

Despite the arguments of some of the rogues in Allen's gang that Hind's action went against all the laws of robbery, the leader was delighted with his protégé, accepted him into the group, and presented him with an excellent horse. Within a short time, the youngster's high spirits and bravery had made him Allen's second lieutenant on their missions of highway robbery. Hind, though, continued to show the same courtesy that had been the hallmark of his first robbery – doffing his hat to his victims while demanding from behind his pistol that they 'stand and deliver'.

The young man was twenty-six and already the subject of numerous tales of robbery when the Civil War broke out. He and the gang had, in the meantime, become masters of deception and disguise: sometimes they would travel in carriages of their own so as to lull the suspicions of other travellers as they approached them; and Hind in particular displayed a skill at disguise, appearing on some occasions dressed as a servant and on others in women's clothing! Yet despite the rich hauls he was making and the comfortable lifestyle he was enjoying, James Hind did not hesitate when war broke out, and at once quit the highway and joined the ranks of the king's army. Here he displayed again the same resourcefulness and bravery which had made him such a successful highwayman, and this was recognized when he was commissioned as a captain.

Although Captain Hind fought with bravery for his king – displaying especial courage in the two months siege of Colchester, from which he only escaped when the town fell on 27 August 1648, by resorting to his skill at disguise and slipping through Cromwell's forces dressed as a woman – he could do nothing to stem the inevitable defeat of the Royalists. When, five months after the siege, Charles was executed, Hind vowed to continue his own private war against the Protector.

Reunited with Thomas Allen and his gang – most of whom had also served the Royalist cause – Hind suggested one of the boldest and most daring schemes in the annals of highway robbery: an attack on the coach of Oliver Cromwell as it journeyed from Huntingdon to London. Although the gang were skilled horsemen and doughty fighters, Cromwell also travelled well protected and the hold-up turned into a débâcle for the outlaws.

Hind and the others took on the coach and its bodyguards with their usual vigour, but they were beaten back without getting anywhere near the hated Protector. Allen, in fact, fell from his horse and was quickly taken prisoner, while three of his men also fell from pistol wounds. Sensing that all was lost, Hind turned from the fray and only just managed to outrun his pursuers before his horse fell, exhausted. His mentor and friend, the unfortunate Thomas Allen, was later tried and hanged at Tyburn.

After the failure of this mission, the Allen gang scattered and Hind decided to continue his career alone. He was soon so successful, in fact, that he became – in the words of another broadsheet – 'a kind of bogey, or will-o'-the-wisp sort of fellow, who could miraculously be in at least two places at one and the same time wherever highway robberies were reported'. Newspaper accounts of his robberies took to calling him, 'that Grand Thief of England', and a rumour grew that he had been given a magic talisman by a witch, which would protect him against capture and injury!

While the captain had no intention of repeating the mistaken attack on Cromwell, he did take particular pleasure in robbing certain other of the Puritan leaders who were foolish enough to use the highways he frequented. A famous story of his encounter with Hugh Peters – the uncrowned archbishop of Commonwealth England, whom Hind held up as he travelled along Enfield Chase in Middlesex – did no harm to his legend whatsoever.

Peters was not a man easily frightened, however, and when Hind appeared from behind a clump of trees demanding that he hand over his valuables, the churchman responded by starting to quote extracts from the Bible at his impudent adversary. 'The Eighth Commandment commands that you should not steal,' Peters declared; 'beside, it is said by Solomon, Rob not the Poor, because he is poor.'

Despite being momentarily taken aback by these words, Hind, who had of course been educated and was reasonably familiar with the Bible, decided to answer in kind. 'Friend,' he replied with a faint smile,

> if you had obeyed God's precepts as you ought, you would not have presumed to have wrested His Holy Word to such an abominable and wicked sense, as thou didst the words of the Prophet when he said, 'Bind their Kings with chains, and their nobles with fetters of iron', to aggravate the misfortunes of your royal master, whom your cursed republican party unjustly murdered before his own palace.

It was now Hugh Peters's turn to be startled at this display of erudition from one he took to be just a common highwayman – but he continued to use the Bible to try and explain both the need for the overthrowing of King Charles and the sinfulness of highway robbery.

Hind listened to the churchman's words for several minutes and then halted him with an angry levelling of his pistol, growling:

> Pray, sir, make no reflection on my profession, when Solomon plainly says, 'Do not despise a thief'. But it is to little purpose for us to dispute – deliver your money or else I shall send thee out of the world to thy master, the Devil, in an instant!

Seeing the anger on Captain Hind's face, the churchman obviously realized his words were falling on deaf ears and hastily handed over thirty pieces of gold. With another wave of his pistol, the highwayman indicated his victim could continue on his way – but before the man was out of sight he had ridden up beside him once more.

This time it was Hugh Peters who could only listen open-mouthed as the highwayman spoke again:

> Sir, now I think on it, this disaster has befallen you because you did not observe that place in the scriptures which says, 'Provide neither gold, nor silver, nor brass, in your purse for your journey.' And truly, sir, you must now pardon me for taking away your cloak and coat, too, because the Scripture says in another place, 'And him that taketh away thy cloak, forbid him not to take away thy coat also'!

It was a cold and dispirited churchman who rode off into the gloom that night with Captain Hind's laughter ringing in his ears. Nor was Hugh Peters's humiliation quite finished, for on the following Sunday he decided to take as the theme of his sermon 'The Sin of Theft' using for his text the verses 'I have put off my coat, how shall I put it on?'

Scarcely, though, had the unfortunate churchman delivered these words from his pulpit than a voice from the back of the congregation was heard to whisper, audibly enough for all those present to hear, 'Upon my word, sir, I can't tell – unless Captain Hind was here!'

The laughter which then greeted this remark – and when gossip carried it across the nation – had hardly subsided before Captain Hind had confronted another Parliamentarian, Serjeant Bradshaw, who had sat in judgement on the king, and was much disliked for his pomposity. He was travelling in his stately carriage when halted by the highwayman on the road between Sherborne and Shaftesbury in Dorsetshire.

Bradshaw, like Hugh Peters, responded to Hind's demand for his valuables by trying to bluff his way out of the situation – asking if the highwayman knew who he was. Captain Hind's temper was obviously on a shorter fuse than previously, for he shouted at the figure peering at him through the coach window:

> Hah! I fear neither you nor any King-killing son of a whore alive! I have now as much power over you as you lately had over the King, and I should do God and my country good service if I made the same use of it; but live villain to suffer the pangs of thine own conscience, till Justice shall lay her iron hand upon thee and require an answer for thy crimes, who are unworthy to die by any hands but those of the common hangman, or at any other place than Tyburn. Therefore if you do not give me your

money instantly, I'll in a moment send you out of the world without any benefit of clergy at all!

Trembling at the vehemence of the robber's words, Bradshaw meekly handed out of the window about forty shillings in silver. Hind took one look at the coins and, knowing full well that the serjeant always travelled with larger sums, threw them back and demanded that unless he produced some gold he would shoot him through the heart. At this, a shaking hand produced a purse full of jacobuses.

Pulling open the purse, Captain Hind allowed a grin of triumph to cross his handsome features.

This, sir, is the metal that wins my heart for ever. O precious gold! I admire and adore thee, as much as either Bradshaw, Prynne or any other villain of the same stamp. This is that incomparable medicament which the republican physicians call the wonder-working plaster. It is truly Catholic in operation, and somewhat akin to the Jesuit's powder, but more effectual. The virtues of it are strange and various; it maketh justice deaf, as well as blind; and takes out spots of the deepest treasons, as easily as Castile soap does common stains. It alters a man's constitution in two or three days, more than the virtuoso's transfusion of blood can do in seven years ... In a word [added the highwayman, now clearly enjoying his own verbosity] it makes fools wise men, and wise men fools, and both of them knaves. The very colour of this precious balm is bright and dazzling. If it be properly applied to the fist, that is, in a decent manner, and in competent dose, it infallibly performs all the cures I have mentioned, and many others too numerous to mention!

Hind stopped to draw breath and then raised his pistols. 'You and your infernal crew have hitherto run on Jehulike, therefore it is time now to stop your career!'

Bradshaw, all his bombast gone and fearing for his life, cowered in the corner of his carriage as shots rang out from the highwayman's pistols. But it was not the passenger he was aiming at – rather the six horses drawing the carriage, and one by one they fell to the ground.

The slaughter may well have been a callous act, but it enabled Captain Hind to escape without danger of immediate pursuit and continue his career. A third member of the hated regicides,

Colonel Harrison, also received the captain's attention on the Bath road near Maidenhead Thicket a little later, where he was relieved of the sum of seventy pounds. However, the colonel instituted a pursuit and Captain Hind was only able to make good his escape thanks to a warning from a friendly innkeeper. During the course of his flight he was also, inadvertently, responsible for killing a man named George Sympson who suddenly appeared galloping along the highway. Wrongly assuming the man was pursuing him, when he was actually trying to catch up his master who had left by coach earlier in the day, the highwayman raised his pistol and shot him dead. It was not until later that Captain Hind was to learn of his mistake ...

Aware, though, that he was now badly wanted by the authorities, the 'Grand Thief' decided to enjoy the proceeds of his robberies for a time, and vowed that when he returned to the road he would steer clear of Cromwell's men. Indeed, his next hold-up marked a return to those earlier exploits that had earned him his reputation for chivalry and kindness.

Despite the vast amounts of money he secured from his robberies, Captain Hind could never keep it long, either spending it lavishly or giving it to those in need. Hence it was not long before Serjeant Bradshaw and Colonel Harrison's gold had run out and the bold highwayman had to take to the road once again. This time he lay in wait on the road between Petersfield and Portsmouth, in Hampshire, and confronted a coach he was surprised and delighted to find was carrying a party of ladies.

Confident that there was no need for any show of strength, Captain Hind merely commanded the coachman to halt and then, sweeping off his hat, bowed to the ladies. Apologizing politely for having interrupted their journey, he explained that it had been necessitated by his love for a member of their fair sex upon whom he had expended all his money. He was, he said, now financially embarrassed and hoped they would be able to replenish his pockets.

In fact, only one of the ladies was carrying any money – she was travelling with her friends to get married and taking her dowry along – the not inconsiderable sum of £3,000. Totally charmed by the dashing highwayman, one of the girls let this fact slip. Ever courteous, Captain Hind replied that though he regretted doing it, he must have some of this money – not all, he insisted, £1,000 would do as he had no desire to ruin the young lady's marriage. And she was to tell her fiancé that the money was only a loan which he would do his best to repay at a later date.

With another bow, the captain rode off, leaving the young women still buzzing about their encounter. Sadly, though, there was an unhappy sequel to this story – for the bridegroom-to-be apparently refused to accept the girl without her dowry in full and called off the marriage. One chronicler of the story conjectured that if the gallant captain had heard of this mercenary attitude he would probably have dealt with the callous young man in a similar manner to Serjeant Bradshaw!

Another example of Captain Hind's generosity of spirit had a happier ending. Learning that an innkeeper in Warwick who had once sheltered him was about to be arrested for failing to pay a fine of twenty pounds, Hind rode to the tavern and gave the man the money to pay the debt. He then, however, lay in wait until the money-lender had collected all his cash and held him up as he was returning home. Not only did he relieve the fellow of the twenty pounds, but demanded a further sum of ten pounds as 'interest'.

Such exploits further enhanced the highwayman's reputation as a kind of latter-day Robin Hood as well as making him one of the most wanted criminals of the time – though it is true to say he preferred rather bigger hauls than this one, declaring his philosophy of robbery in these words: 'Disgrace not yourselves for small sums, but aim high, and for great ones, for the least will bring you to the gallows.'

In truth, though he was still only in his early thirties, the remarkable career of Captain Hind was about to draw to a perhaps predictable close.

Like Moll Cutpurse and the other Royalist supporters, Captain Hind wanted to see the monarchy restored, and in 1650 he travelled to Scotland to offer his services to the young Prince Charles living in exile there. His reputation had apparently gone before him and, after an audience with the prince, he was welcomed into the Royalist army, which set out for London the following year. The notorious Battle of Worcester that followed saw not only the rout of Charles's forces and his narrow escape to France after hiding in an oak tree, but also the ruination of Captain Hind's hopes. He similarly only escaped capture by the skin of his teeth.

Perhaps not surprisingly, Hind returned to his old haunts in London and, after staying for a time with Moll Cutpurse, found more permanent lodgings above a barber's shop in Fleet Street where he lived under the innocuous name of James Brown. But it was no doubt difficult for a man of his looks and character to keep his identity secret, and in November 1651 he was betrayed by an associate and arrested on a charge of armed robbery.

News of the famous Captain Hind's capture caused a sensation, and when he was brought to the Old Bailey for trial on 12 December, huge crowds gathered to catch a glimpse of him. The Roundhead authorities, who were anxious not to turn the dashing highwayman into a Cavalier martyr, soon found themselves embarrassed still further when a lack of both evidence and prosecution witnesses forced them to drop the case! What, though, seems in hindsight particularly strange about this situation is why Hugh Peters, Serjeant Bradshaw and Colonel Harrison, the three Parliamentarian bigwigs who had been so rudely treated by the captain, did not come forward to testify.

For three months Hind was held in Newgate while the authorities debated what to do with him. In the interim, he became still more of a public favourite, receiving hordes of visitors in his cell, and finding himself the subject of all manner of publications. Then, in March 1652, he was taken to Reading and charged with the murder of the unfortunate servant George Sympson. But even though he was found guilty, Cromwell had just passed a new act, the Act of Oblivion, which prevented the hanging of criminals for all but one charge – that of high treason. The captain could breath again.

But when he was moved a third time and taken to Worcester assizes there was to be no case of third time lucky. For he had made no secret of his part in the battle against the Parliamentarian forces which had taken place near the city and was duly charged with high treason. Entering the witness box to face cross-examination, Hind once again displayed the same bravado he had shown on the highways, declaring with a smile,

> Well, I value it not three pence to lose my life in a good cause. I owe a debt to God and a debt I must pay. Blessed be His name, that He hath kept me from shedding blood unjustly, which is now a great comfort to me. Neither have I wronged any poor

> man of the worth of a penny, but I must confess that I have, when I have been necessitated to, made bold with a rich bumpkin or a lying lawyer, whose full-fed fees from the rich farmer doth too much impoverish the poor cottage keeper.

Hind continued to taunt his accusers with the same smile and gentle impudence, as the crowded public galleries shook with laughter and applauded his wit. But there was no saving him from the law and he was duly found guilty of high treason and sentenced to death.

And so the first major highwayman in history, barely thirty-four years old, finally went to his death on 24 September 1652 with a characteristic wave of his hand and a doff of his hat, before suffering the terrible fate of being hanged, drawn and quartered outside Worcester Gaol. There were those present who said afterwards that they could swear there was still a smile on his severed head when it was placed midway across the Severn Bridge.

The captain might indeed have been dead, but his legend was only just beginning – and far from having put a stop to rogues like him, the authorities now found that many more were plundering the highways of England. The arrest of two suspected highwaymen, reported in the newspapers only a few days before the captain was executed, bore vivid testimony to this fact. 'They will not confess their names', the newspaper stated, 'and therefore are supposed to be gentleman of quality, and it is conceived they are of the knot of Captain Hind, that grand thief of England, that hath his associates upon all roads.'

In truth, though the 'Grand Thief' had shouted his last 'Stand and deliver!', there were plenty more highwaymen riding in his place: the good, the bad *and* the absurd, as the next chapter will reveal …

4 'The Wild Sons of Gentlemen'

There are actually very few records of highwaymen before the start of the seventeenth century, although historians are agreed that travellers were being stopped and robbed of their valuables on isolated stretches of road during the two closing decades of the previous century.

One of the earliest recorded instances dates from 1585 and notes the execution at York Castle of one Henry William Genyembre 'for robbery on the Queen's highway'. It would be interesting to know more of this strange case for Genyembre had come from a good background, but was well known as a horse-thief and by the time he held up and relieved a traveller of his watch and twenty pounds in gold coins he was said to be 'a man advanced in years'!

Also from Yorkshire, there is another account of two highwaymen, both much younger blades in their twenties, who suffered the same punishment some five years later for carrying out a robbery on the road between York and Hull. According to historian Arthur Griffiths in *Mysteries of Police and Crime* (1905), 'Highway robbery was much practised in Yorkshire and the north at that time, when Amos Lawson and Ebenizer Moor were noted gentlemen of the road.'

There is, unfortunately, a lack of evidence to support this contention and no more details about Lawson and Moor, the 'noted gentlemen of the road'. But there *is* a rather more full account of a highway robbery committed on the person of the Earl of Dumfries in 1592.

The nobleman was travelling along the famous Great North Road between Lincoln and Bawtry when he was forced to halt by two well-dressed fellows later identified as Nicholas Spavild and Richard Drew. The earl reported in his deposition that the men 'sett upon him and demanded from him one bay mare and a black nagg with a great lether mail full of goods. Thereupon he was forced to go to Bawtry on foot and there raysed the hue and cry after them.'

Spavild and Drew were obviously inexperienced highwaymen for they were caught within hours, and offered a preposterous defence for their action, made note of in court records. The pair claimed that they had seen the gentleman 'riding off the road and over corn' and when they had approached him he had dismounted and 'taking his servant with him had left his horses which they had carried off intending to take them to the pound'. Their story notwithstanding, Spavild and Drew were summarily hanged.

That highwaymen were known in Elizabethan times is, though, further confirmed by Shakespeare in *Henry IV, Part I* where their activities are regarded as fair sport when Falstaff suggests that Prince Hal should join him in a robbery on Gads Hill.

'Who, I rob?' the prince declares. 'I a thief? Not I, by my faith.'

To which Falstaff rejoins, 'There's neither honesty, manhood, nor good fellowship in thee, nor thou camest not of the blood royal, if thou darest not stand for ten shillings.'

Won over by this argument, the prince agrees that 'once in my days I'll be a madcap.'

Shakespeare was probably only mirroring the tolerant attitude of many members of the general public towards highway robbery, although, as it was only the well-off who fell prey to these 'madcaps', the attitude is more understandable.

The Bard refers to highwaymen in several other of his plays, but provides no clues as to the prototypes of his outlaws of the road. Indeed, it is not until 1605, when the reputation of young Moll Cutpurse was already the talk of London, that what is generally regarded as the first full-length history of a highwayman was published. This was entitled *The Life and Death of Gamaliel Ratsey* and, thanks to a copy having survived, which now resides in the Bodleian Library in Oxford, it has been possible to extract from it the pertinent details for this study.

It has to be admitted that there is not a great deal of evidence to support the highly colourful account of this strangely named man's life, and some historians feel much of it may be a figment of the anonymous author's imagination. Be that as it may, Gamaliel Ratsey 'a famous thiefe in England executed at Bedford the 26 of March last past, 1605' – to quote the book's title-page – can certainly be viewed as typical of the earliest highwayman, if not a kind of composite of them all.

The 'facts' of the book are these. Gamaliel was apparently born at Market Deeping in Lincolnshire (though no date is given) the son of a well-to-do gentleman, Richard Ratsey, who was in the service of a local nobleman. The boy was given a good education, but proved of 'a roving disposition' and in the year 1600 (the first date provided) was in Ireland serving in the army of occupation under the Earl of Essex. The young man so distinguished himself, the book claims, that when he returned to Market Deeping he had been promoted to the rank of sergeant.

But the quiet life of Lincolnshire seems not to have suited his tastes for within a matter of months he had 'begun a career of filching', culminating in stealing forty pounds in gold coins from the landlady of a tavern in Spalding. The crime was quickly traced to Ratsey, however, and he was arrested and condemned to hang.

A short and undistinguished career could well have ended there, but for the fact that young Gamaliel showed a degree of resourcefulness by breaking out of the gaol where he was being held and running off into the night. It was as well he soon fell into the company of a pair of itinerant rogues – named only as Snell and Shorthouse – who happened to be in the neighbourhood, because he had escaped wearing only his shirt!

This trio decided to make their living on the highway and were soon holding up travellers along the roads of East Anglia. The book claims that on one occasion the three men successfully robbed a company of nine men of several thousand pounds. Some of the proceeds from these hold-ups, it adds in rather grandiloquent terms, were later generously bestowed upon the poor of the district!

Gamaliel Ratsey is also accorded the distinction of having been the first highwayman to make a special mask which covered his entire face. Although this made his features indistinguishable, the mask was apparently so horrible as to frighten his victims more than the pistols he was waving under their noses! The legend of this mask so intrigued the dramatist Ben Jonson (himself to be a highway victim, as we shall see) that in his play *The Alchemist*, first produced in 1610, he refers to one of the characters as having a 'face cast worse than Gamaliel Ratsey's!'

The highwayman's biography further describes him as a man with a crude sense of humour who, if he happened to stop penniless travellers, would humiliate them in some way. An actor he held up near Norwich was forced to play a scene from *Hamlet*, while a scholar stopped on the road to Cambridge was made to recite a learned thesis.

Such stories, though, are believed to have been lifted from earlier legends to embellish Ratsey's life – though the details of his end seem less open to doubt. Snell and Shorthouse were apparently captured after a robbery early in 1605 and endeavoured to save their own necks by turning King's Evidence and giving away the whereabouts of the other member of their trio. Gamaliel was therefore soon arrested and hanged at Bedford on 26 March.

According to records at the Bodleian Library, the biography of this ingenious if rather unsavoury highwayman was published just a month after he had swung – and such was the success of the publication that a rival London publisher issued a supposed sequel later in the month entitled *Ratsey's Ghoste; or, The Second Part of his Madde Pranks and Robberies*. This stretched the improbabilities of the first work into the realms of the impossible, though again it was popular and undoubtedly increased the public fascination with the growing number of highwaymen now about their roads …

A surprising fact which soon becomes apparent when examining the information about these early members of the fraternity is that many came from good backgrounds. While it is certainly true that much of the British criminal class at this time still came from the big city slums or impoverished rural communities – that is, the pick-pockets, house-breakers and footpads – the swelling band of highway robbers were, with few exceptions, the sons of gentlemen. Of course, the horse and weapons which were an essential part of the highwayman's equipment were beyond the means of the poorer criminals, but this is by no means the only explanation for the phenomenon.

The beginning of the age of the highwayman coincided, in fact, with two major developments which occurred in the years just prior to the Civil War: an increase in the number of travellers on the country's roads and the improvement in the design of portable weapons like the pistol. What turned the sons of good families to crime was a combination of a desire for adventure and excitement and a – perhaps more pressing – need for money to pay their debts – especially those incurred through gambling and high living.

It is perhaps not surprising, therefore, to find that these men were well dressed, well armed and deserved the epithet of 'the wild sons of gentlemen'. There are three outstanding examples from the early years of Charles I's reign which may suffice for the whole fraternity.

An archetype of these highwaymen was surely Walter Tracey, born in 1596, and described thus by Captain Alexander Smith:

> He was the younger son of a gentleman, worth £900 per annum, in Norfolk, and had a liberal education bestowed upon him at King's College in Cambridge, but living not within the bounds of £120, which his father left him, he would often go out and take a purse on the highway.

Tracey was evidently a handsome young man with a smooth tongue who had begun drinking and gambling heavily while still at university. When he added seduction to his curriculum and was found out, he was promptly dismissed from Cambridge in disgrace. His father's plans for him to enter the church were naturally abandoned in favour of removing him to Cheshire where he was set to work for a wealthy grazier.

To his looks Walter could add charming manners and musical skills and he used these to good effect when he set about seducing the local female population, as Smith has also reported:

> Being a handsome man he much indicted himself to the intrigues of love, so that when occasion did sometimes present itself to taste a little of the sweet pleasures of nature, he was not so scrupulous to believe he offended the laws of God nor man, in the enjoyment of maid, wife or widow, in the dalliance of unlawful sports.

Skilled though Tracey became at seducing country females – including the grazier's own wife, who also fell for his 'tongue-padding, in which he had a good facility', according to another report – the young man soon began to tire of the country life and, stealing the grazier's wallet, containing eighty pounds, to see him on his way, he set off for London.

In the big city, however, Tracey quickly learned he was not quite as clever as he believed himself to be, when a new acquaintance swindled him out of all the money he had stolen. Now penniless, and realizing he could expect no help from his father, he decided to become a highwayman. The first hold-up he committed was to provide another salutory lesson.

According to legend, Walter Tracey waylaid near Puckeridge, Hertfordshire, a student who was on his way to Cambridge. At pistol-point, the man admitted he was carrying sixty pounds in a portmanteau which was to pay for his expenses while he took his MA degree. He begged and pleaded with Tracey not to take his money – or at least to leave him with something to be going on with.

At this – the story goes – the highwayman revealed an element of generosity in his character and took four pounds from his own pocket and handed it to his victim as he snatched the man's bag. With a flourish, Tracey then reared his horse and shouted back at his victim as he rode away, 'That will carry you very well to Cambridge, friend, and there tell your Collegians you met with a very honest highwayman!'

Some miles on, Tracey stopped to open the student's bag and count his money. He realized the cost of his 'generosity' at once – for inside he found not the gold coins he had expected, but a jumble of old and worn clothing, 'which set him a-swearing and cursing like a devil to think that he should be such a damned fool as to give £4 for that which was not worth twenty shillings', Smith's account adds.

Walter Tracey had, though, learned his lesson, for there were to be no more such examples of kindness shown during his career of crime on the road. Among his victims was the aforementioned Ben Jonson whom he held up near Beaconsfield in Buckinghamshire. When Jonson likewise tried to dissuade Tracey from robbing him with a poetic appeal which began, 'Fly villain hence, or by the coat of steel I'll make thy heart my leaden bullet feel', the university-educated highwayman replied in kind:

> Art thou great Ben? Or the revived ghost
> Of famous Shakespeare? Or some drunken host

Who being tipsy with thy muddy beer,
Dost think thy rhymes will daunt my soul with fear?
Nay, know base slave, that I am one of those
Can take a purse as well in verse as prose;
And when thou'rt dead, write this upon thy hearse:
Here lies a poet who was robbed in verse.

Apocryphal though this exchange of verse may be, Tracey certainly had the drop on Jonson and convinced him he was best advised to hand over his purse. And making doubly sure he was not about to be cheated a second time, Walter checked the contents and, finding ten gold jacobuses therein, rode off happily.

Records indicate that this highwayman enjoyed several years of uninterrupted success, although his passion for the opposite sex regularly emptied his pockets as well as putting him in increasing danger of arrest. Then, in 1634, apparently determined to make one big 'killing', he attempted to rob the Duke of Buckingham as he was travelling to Portsmouth. Instead, however, he was overwhelmed by the nobleman's bodyguards and arrested.

In May of that year, Walter Tracey, gentleman's son and man of the road, was tried and found guilty at Winchester. He was summarily hanged, aged thirty-eight years.

The career of the second of the trio of early highwaymen, John Clavel – a contemporary of Tracey – who was the nephew and heir of Sir William Clavel, a Dorsetshire squire, is also similarly well documented – though it was considerably shorter in duration.

The Clavels, who could trace their lineage back to the days of William the Conqueror, were, at first glance, an unlikely family to have provided what Charles Harper has called 'one of the really notable highwaymen of the early years of the seventeenth century'. Yet the historian sees the explanation for his having pursued this career as quite simply because 'he was one among those younger sons and expectant heirs who, however great were their expectations in some more or less remote future, were generally, in the present tense, not only poor, but head over ears in debt'.

What makes John Clavel even more interesting is that, like Tracey, he was something of a poet, and was, additionally, a writer who, after his arrest, wrote in prison an autobiography which he entitled *Recantation of an Ill-led Life.* A surviving copy once again provides us with the basic information of his life and times in crime.

John Clavel was born in 1603 at the family manor of Smedmore on the Dorset coast. A high-spirited and adventurous lad, he was educated by a tutor but turned to crime before reaching his majority and was promptly disowned by his family. John's first act of highway robbery was apparently no more than a prank directed against an aged traveller on a lonely Dorset road, but the thrill so excited him that he felt compelled to carry out more of the same, most at night.

According to his *Recantation*, Clavel became 'a thorough-paced highwayman, deep in the counsels of the high-toby gloats and a past master in all their devices.' Among the locations he worked were Gads Hill and Shooters Hill on the outskirts of London, though by his own admission he made his best pickings holding up mail-coaches on the Dover road.

Clavel seemingly adopted a variety of disguises to carry out his robberies, including hoods, masks, eye-patches, false beards and even an artificial nose. He was sheltered by a number of landlords upon whom he lavished gifts of money and valuables to buy their silence. Yet none of these artifices could prevent his arrest in 1626 when he was just twenty-three years old. An account in the *News Letter* of 11 February reports:

> Mr. Clavell, a gentleman, a knight's eldest son, a great highway robber, and of posts, was, together with a soldier, his companion, arraigned and condemned, on Monday last, at the King's Bench bar. He pleaded for himself that he had never struck or wounded any man, had never taken anything from their bodies, as rings, etc., never cut their girths or saddles, or done them, when he robbed, any corporeal violence. He was, with his companion, sentenced to death, but after an appeal to His Majesty, the King, he has been reprieved.

This successful 'appeal', it transpires, was rather more unusual than most, for it was couched in verse and read as follows:

> I that have robb'd so oft, am now bid stand;
> Death and the law assault me, and demand

My life and means. I never used men so;
But having ta'en their money, let them go.
Yet must I die! And is there no reliefe?
The King of Kings had mercy on a thiefe!
So may our gracious King too, if he please,
Without his council, grant me a release.
God is his precedent, and men shall see
His mercy goe beyond severity.

Whether King Charles was flattered by this grovelling apology or whether – as has been suggested – Clavel's influential family were able to buy his release from death: reprieves were granted to both John and his accomplice, and their sentences commuted to life imprisonment.

Having found that his pen had saved him from the gallows, Clavel now determined to employ it to get him set free, and in October 1627 he published his pamphlet – much of it again in verse – *Recantation of an Ill-led Life*. Not surprisingly, it was dedicated to the king along with a lengthy list of other important figures whom the author undoubtedly hoped to impress. What, putting aside its rather nauseating self-justification, makes the pamphlet important, is the insight it gives into the *modus operandi* of highwaymen, written as it was by someone with first-hand knowledge. It also contained detailed information addressed to the public on how they might spot and help arrest highwaymen!

The pamphlet was obviously a success with the public – it ran to at least three editions – but whether it was purchased as a curiosity or as a practical guide to travelling on the highways, can only be conjectured. Some of the chapter-headings, though, provide a flavour of Clavel's manual of highway robbery: 'How as he rides a man shall know a thief from an honest man'; 'How soon the highwaymen spend what unlawfully they get'; 'The Danger of travelling on the Sabbath Day'; 'Being Robbed, how to follow and which way to set forth the Hue and Cry'; 'When To Ride', 'Where To Ride', and 'How To Ride'; plus what was obviously intended to be a comforting final note: 'If by chance the traveller is beset, how to behave himself'!

It was Clavel himself, though, who was to enjoy the biggest surprise, for he became one of the very rare exceptions among highwaymen to be given a royal pardon and set free. What happened to him after his release is, however, somewhat shrouded in mystery.

One source claims that when Clavel was turned away from his family home he returned to a life on the road and was soon after shot and killed by a quick-witted traveller he attempted to rob. Another authority believes he joined the army and died in 1628 during Charles's inglorious war against France.

A third story, carried as an addendum in the last edition of his *Recantation*, published in 1629, claims that Clavel had actually been as good as his promises and, following his release from prison, had gone into the country to live quietly enjoying 'a most singular reformation'. True or not, this singular man had certainly left his mark on the history of highway robbery.

The third of the trio of gentleman highwaymen was Isaac Atkinson, the son of a Berkshire squire who also had enjoyed a good upbringing but had fallen into bad ways by the time he was a teenager.

Born in 1614 on the family estate at Farringdon, he began a course of rebellion against authority, mixed with the pursuit of vice, no sooner than his father had sent him to Brasenose College, Oxford, at the age of sixteen. The boy would undoubtedly have come into a comfortable fortune had he followed his father's intention that he should run the estate, but, after being thrown out of university for his waywardness, he was soon in even greater trouble, seducing the local womenfolk. According to one account:

> Not a maidservant could live with the old gentleman for the son's importunities, unless she gave up her honour to his desires. Not a handsome wife or daughter in the neighbourhood but either submitted to his pleasure or complained of him to his father.

After Isaac had fathered several illegitimate children and tried his parents' patience beyond breaking point, he was disinherited and thrown out of the family home. Highway robbery provided the only opening for his 'talents', he decided.

Atkinson's first venture into crime was to break into the house of a certain earl whom he, by chance, came across in bed having sex with his wife. What happened next has been amusingly recorded by Captain Alexander Smith:

> Isaac arrived at the critical minute as his lordship was performing the family duty and heard him say whilst they were at generation work, 'I vow, Madam, I have five hundred pounds lying over the

> bed's tester, which I would give with all my heart to a surgeon who could rectify a mistake which Nature hath made with you.

It was all young Isaac could do to restrain his laughter as he hid behind the bedroom curtains, but he was also hardly able to believe his good luck. He remained concealed where he was until the couple were asleep and then stole away with the money that had been so incautiously revealed to him.

Before the following day was over Isaac Atkinson had purchased a horse and a good pair of pistols, ridden to London, and begun to make his plans for further criminal ventures – once, of course, his windfall was spent.

Records indicate that Atkinson became a cold and calculating highway robber – on one occasion taking silver and valuables from a preacher whose Sunday service he had earlier attended in Uxbridge; and on another, holding up William Noy, none other than the king's Attorney-General, from whom he extracted a purse of gold at pistol-point.

In fact, Atkinson seems to have had a predilection for men of the law. As Captain Alexander Smith has written, in claiming even greater triumphs for him:

> He was the greatest plague to the lawyers of any highwayman that ever was in England, for he had the impudence to ride to all the circuits over the Kingdom, so that many of that profession often became his prey. And one time in less than eight months he robbed above 160 attorneys in the county of Norfolk, from whom he took upwards of £3,000. This audacious robber was a man of undaunted spirit and would assault one, two, three, four or five men himself.

Although this claim seems rather improbable, it *was* a fact that lawyers were among the favourite targets for highwaymen. What is, though, beyond dispute is that it was Atkinson's weakness for a pretty face that brought about the end of his career.

In the summer of 1640 he was riding along a road near Turnham Green when he came across a young woman on horseback returning from market with a bag, obviously containing money, slung around her waist. Engaging her in conversation, the young highwayman soon began to think of seducing the girl before taking her money. She, though, was not so easily fooled and, suddenly hurling the bag over a nearby hedge, rode off.

With a shrug of his shoulders and the realization that his lust had been frustrated, Atkinson dismounted and decided to make do with the money instead. As he began to search for the bag, however, his stallion which had been attracted to the mare the girl was riding, took off in pursuit of its quarry.

A double blow awaited Atkinson as he watched his mount gallop off. The purse, when found, proved to hold only a large number of halfpences worth no more than forty shillings, while in his own saddle-bag had been nestling gold to the value of eighty guineas! Nor was this the end of his misfortunes – for when the stallion caught up with the girl at the Red Lion Inn at Brentford and she realized her assailant must now be on foot, she swiftly organized a search party who galloped back along the road.

It did not take the group long to find Atkinson, vainly trying to make his escape on foot, and though the highwayman shot four men before his bullets ran out, the sheer weight of numbers finally overpowered him. Thereafter he was conveyed to Newgate, tried and condemned to hang at Tyburn. He was just twenty-six years old when he took the last step into oblivion.

Although he did not know it, Atkinson was virtually the last of his kind of highwaymen, 'the wild sons of gentlemen'. The Civil War was less than two years away, and both during and after this conflict a new breed of knights of the road, many of them Cavaliers, were to arise and take up their pistols seeking revenge on the nation's oppressors as well as lining their pockets. With his dying words, Atkinson seemed to herald this new era. 'There's nothing,' he shouted as the rope was placed around his neck and pulled tight, 'nothing like a merry life and a short one!'

5 The Knights of the Road

The civil war which broke out in England in August 1642, setting Charles I and his Royalist supporters against the Parliamentarians lead by Oliver Cromwell and his Roundheads, put a temporary stop to the activities of most highwaymen. The reason for this was quite simple – almost all of them were fanatical followers of the king and offered their services to his cause. To the cynical amongst them, of course, a monarchy also represented a wealthy travelling aristocracy, while the Puritans promised only austerity and, inevitably, fewer rich pickings.

In the important battles of the war – such as Edgehill (23 October 1642), Marston Moor (2 July 1644) and Naseby (14 June 1645) – men who had once held travellers to ransom on the country's roads now levelled their pistols against Cromwell's forces. Though the Parliamentarians won the day – as indeed they continued to do when a second rising of Royalist and Presbyterian forces was put down in the summer of 1648 – the spirit of those highwaymen-turned-Cavaliers who survived was not diminished, and it is no surprise to learn that many returned to their old habits.

In most cases these men had no option but to turn to crime, having lost their estates and fortunes to the Parliamentarians; but some simply preferred the old life and the chance it offered – small though it might be – for revenge against the authorities. Historian Patrick Pringle has neatly summarized the state of affairs at this moment in time, in *Stand and Deliver: The Story of the Highwaymen* (1951).

> When the War was over the highwaymen went back to the roads and had to make the best of it. Some of the old-timers had been killed fighting for the King, but their ranks had been greatly increased as a result of the War. Not only did many disbanded

> Royalist soldiers turn to the road as the only means of making a livelihood, but there were ex-officers among them, too. Dispossessed and often with a price on their heads, many a gallant Captain – and even higher ranks – spent the time waiting for the Restoration as knights of the road.

The records of the period make it plain that these 'knights of the road' were battle-hardened fighters skilled in the use of military tactics of surprise and hit-and-run skirmishes – ideal strategies for a highwayman. Indeed, by September 1649, they had become so formidable that the Roundhead Commander-in-Chief, General Thomas Fairfax, found it necessary to issue a proclamation to his forces urging them to increase their activity in apprehending highway robbers and promising large rewards for those who were captured. A satirical Royalist publication, *The Man in the Moon*, could not resist having a little fun at this announcement, declaring that the 'House of Robbers' (the House of Commons) had voted for the next six months a reward of ten pounds for the taking of every highway robber, 'the State's officers exempted', it quipped.

But the 'knights', made of sterner stuff, were not to be intimidated by having prices put on their heads. In fact, there was to be no let-up in their activities, and the well-documented stories of a quartet of former Royalist captains whose adventures were the subject of much public gossip and not a little coverage in print will serve to represent many other such cases.

What linked all these men were their clothing (all wore the legendary uniform of cocked hat, embroidered frock-coat and thigh-length leather boots), their impeccable manners, and their consideration for their victims. Violence was rarely perpetrated on those who complied with the highwaymen's instructions; pistols were only fired if real danger presented itself; and not a few of the robbers would shake the hands of male victims and kiss the fingers of ladies before riding off with their spoils.

Perhaps the best known of these men was Captain Philip Stafford, a handsome young fellow born in 1622, the only son of a gentleman farmer of Newbury, Berkshire. As a child, Stafford had become an excellent rider and shot, and, sharing his aged father's admiration for the king, he volunteered his services when barely twenty years old. His bravery in battle lead to his being commissioned and he would surely have risen higher in the ranks of the Royalist army had it not been defeated. He was forced to flee for his life. Finding that his patrimony had been sequestered and he was now penniless, the Cavalier decided to turn to highway robbery.

According to contemporary accounts, Captain Stafford chose as his principal area of operations the spot known as Maidenhead Thicket in Berkshire. Apart from lifting a considerable amount of jewellery from rich female travellers, he also vented his particular dislike of nonconformist ministers by robbing several of them of their cash. It is said that in time he amassed a considerable sum of money and decided to leave the road and retire to a village in the north of Yorkshire.

A colourful account of the captain's life claims that in time he became a lay-preacher in the rural community, and when the previous minister died he was 'elected in the good man's stead and acquitted himself to the entire satisfaction of the people'. They must have been less than satisfied, though, when Stafford was reported missing one morning – along with all the church's silver-plate!

Whether there is any truth in this story or not, Captain Stafford did return to highway robbery, but seemingly acted with less care than before. In 1649 he robbed a farmer of thirty-three pounds on the road to Reading, but was so lackadaisical in making his getaway that two well-armed local men sent on his trail had him in custody within an hour. A week later he was tried at Reading assizes and sentenced to be hanged.

The captain, however, met his fate with courage and some style. He was allowed to live in prison in a manner befitting someone of his rank and was visited by a couple of other members of the highway fraternity who began to work out a plan to help him escape. When a whisper of this plot reached the authorities, however, the date of his execution was brought forward. Realizing there was now no escape for him, Stafford determined to die as a true knight of the road. Before the day of his hanging he also wrote a short account of his adventures, dwelling on the losses he had sustained in the service of the king and declaring that he had been justified in doing all he had done.

Dressed, according to a contemporary newspaper account, in 'a fine, light coloured suit of clothes with a nosegay on his breast', he looked more like a man going to a fashionable party than his death. On the road from Reading to the gallows he asked permission of his gaolers to halt at a wayside tavern so that he might have a last drink. The politeness of his request won over the men and they agreed.

Doffing his hat to the landlord, Stafford promised he would pay for the drink 'On my way back!' – a joke that so caught the public's imagination, not to mention that of other highwaymen, that it later became something of a ritual with many condemned men of the road going to their executions.

A second Cavalier captain, John Reynolds, met his death with similar panache. Reynolds had been born sometime in the second decade of the century, the son of a wealthy Bristol merchant. He was well educated, spoke several languages and would probably have gone into the family business but for the outbreak of the Civil War. Like Stafford, he rose swiftly to the rank of captain and records show that he was one 'of the King's party in Cornwall, at the disbanding of Lord Hopton's army at Truro'.

Later, with a price on his head, Captain Reynolds took to the roads of south-west England and began holding up travellers and mail-coaches. He is believed to have been sheltered near Bridgewater by a loyalist farmer, whose daughter he married and had a child with during this time.

Tragically, though, soldiers in the nearby garrison town got to hear rumours of Reynolds's activities, and anxious to cash in on General Fairfax's promise of a reward for any arrested highwayman, they seized the bold Cavalier as he was returning to the farm. In his saddle-bag was all the evidence that was needed to show he had recently committed a successful hold-up.

Reynolds was taken in chains to London to be tried, and there sentenced to hang at Tyburn. On 24 December, along with twenty-eight other criminals – mostly burglers and pick-pockets, although a handful had also committed highway robbery – he was transported to his execution by cart through the streets of the city.

The captain was wearing his Cavalier outfit, and, an eye-witness said afterwards, 'his carriage was very bold' when he approached the hangman. The report added with a flourish, 'As he was going to be turned off, he cried, "God bless King Charles – *Vive le Roi*!" '

Captain Zachary Howard was, if anything, an even more devoted servant of the king. Born in 1620, he had inherited an estate in Glamorganshire worth £1,400 per annum, and enjoyed the indolent life of a rich man; but as soon as the war had broken out he had immediately mortgaged this for £20,000 and used the money to raise a troop of horse for Charles. He was rewarded with the rank of captain, but was forced into exile, returning to England with Charles II to fight at the Battle of Worcester. Following this unsuccessful mission, however, and now with a price on his head, the penniless captain decided that the life of a 'knight of the road' was for him.

Aside from Zachary Howard's determination to rob only those whom he felt represented 'the enemy' – the supporters of Cromwell – he displayed a boldness and audacity in selecting his victims which, not surprisingly, made him something of a folk hero. Among his earliest victims was the Earl of Essex, one of Cromwell's right-hand men, whom the captain held up on Bagshot Heath in Surrey. Despite the fact the earl had six men in attendance, not one of them was prepared to challenge the masked Cavalier with his two glinting pistols, and Howard made off with over £1,200 in gold coins.

His next victim was another nobleman, the Earl of Portsmouth, whom he held up on the outskirts of London. Although the earl was only accompanied by one servant, a contemporary report says that he tried to defy Captain Howard's demand for his valuables – obviously having no knowledge of who the robber was nor of the earlier hold-up.

'You seem by your swearing to be a ranting Cavalier,' the earl declared. 'Have you taken a lease of your life, sir, that you dare venture it against two men?'

Captain Howard threw back his head and roared with laughter. 'I would venture it against ten men, with your idol Cromwell at the head of you!' he said.

No sooner had Howard collected a purse of gold, than he decided to have a little fun at the earl's expense. Making the nobleman get down from his horse, he then had him mount up behind his servant – facing backwards – and bound the two men together, back to back. Having secured the pair, Captain Howard slapped the horse's flank and watched the helpless nobleman's face staring back furiously at him as the animal galloped off into the distance.

The captain behaved even more audaciously when he learned of a consignment of valuables being sent to another of

Cromwell's top men, General Fairfax. The consignment was actually being dispatched to the general's wife with a message, and when the Cavalier had taken possession of this, he decided to present the letter himself.

On receiving the message, and obviously unaware of whom she was talking to, Lady Fairfax asked Howard what had happened to the valuables which were supposed to be accompanying the letter. In his most charming manner, the captain explained that because of fears about a highwayman in the neighbourhood it had been lodged with an innkeeper and he was to go back and collect it when the danger was over. Completely taken in by this story, Lady Fairfax invited the 'messenger' to stay in her house until the time was ripe. Howard was only too happy to accept, for another idea had already crossed his mind.

Given a bed in the servants' quarters, Howard waited until everyone was asleep then slipped quietly upstairs to where Lady Fairfax and her beautiful teenage daughter were sleeping. According to a contemporary report, he then 'ravished them both, beginning with the daughter'.

Just how unwelcome the handsome Cavalier was in the beds of these two ladies it is difficult to tell – for the fact remains that no hue and cry was set up until several hours after he had left the house. He also had the time to take a selection of the Fairfax valuables for good measure!

When General Fairfax returned, then, he had two reasons for feeling aggrieved – but he still only put what must have seemed a rather parsimonious price of £500 on the captain's head ... though by then Howard was well on his way to Ireland, in any case! When he returned to England the next year he had a yet more audacious plan up his sleeve – a plan which involved no less a person than Oliver Cromwell himself.

Captain Howard contrived to stay at the same hotel as Cromwell in Chester and there ingratiated himself into the great man's company. Convincing Cromwell that he, too, was a man of religion, the highwayman was invited to join the Protector at his evening prayers. No sooner had this begun, though, than Captain Howard presented a loaded pistol at Cromwell and bound and gagged him. Then, after taking a few valuables and, according to a contemporary chronicle, 'emptying a chamber pot upon the Protector's head', the captain made good his escape through a window and disappeared into the night.

There was really no way that Howard could top this daring exploit, and it was perhaps sadly inevitable that in 1652 he was captured on the Dover road after attempting to hold up a coach in which six Parliamentarians were travelling. These men reacted instantly and unexpectedly to the lone Cavalier's call to 'Stand and deliver!', and, after a fierce encounter, Howard was overwhelmed by sheer weight of numbers and carried off to Maidstone Gaol.

The trial of Captain Zachary Howard was short and to the point. The evidence given by his long trail of victims made the death sentence inevitable. One of these victims, Oliver Cromwell, is said to have visited the highwayman while he was in prison awaiting execution – unfortunately there is no record of their conversation, which must surely have been fascinating!

Like his fellow Cavalier, Captain Stafford, Howard also met his end with a smile and the cheery exultation of his sovereign.

The fourth of our quartet of 'knights of the road', Captain Thomas Horne, also took part in a robbery of Oliver Cromwell. However, as he was almost immediately captured and hanged, it is his associate, John Cottington (who escaped and became something of a legend under his nickname 'Mulled Sack') who is rather better remembered.

Horne was the son of a prosperous London pewter merchant, had been educated in Europe and was about to join the family business when the Civil War broke out. Urged on by his father, who apparently had connections with the court of Charles I, young Thomas joined Colonel Downe's regiment and was promoted to captain after the first battle of Edgehill.

Like all the other Cavaliers at this time, Captain Horne was left ruined after Cromwell's rise to power and took to the road to support himself, as well as to vent his anger against the powerful figures of the Commonwealth. In 1653 he fell into company with John Cottington and the two men hatched their plot to rob the Protector.

Cottington was an interesting man, the son of a haberdasher in Cheapside, London, who had lost his money and business through drink, and left an impoverished family of nineteen, of which John was the youngest member. Until his early teens, John worked as a chimney-sweep, but became more attracted to the easier money to be had by picking pockets. This also gave him the cash to satisfy a taste for drink which he had obviously inherited from his father. His love of warm, mulled sherry was to earn him his famous nickname.

Despite his impoverished background, 'Mulled Sack' was nevertheless a staunch Royalist, and amongst the people his nimble fingers robbed was the aforementioned Lady Fairfax, who was relieved of a gold watch studded with diamonds as she was going to St Martin's Church near Ludgate Circus. However, when John was caught while trying to pick Oliver Cromwell's pockets as he came out of parliament, the youngster only escaped the death sentence because of a lack of conclusive evidence. He did, however, decide to quit the city and become a highwayman. To make himself appear like the other members of the fraternity John 'disguised himself as a Cavalier in rich apparel' (to quote a contemporary report).

Because of his inexperience, 'Mulled Sack' wisely decided to team up with a veteran highwayman named Tom Cheney, and the pair took to holding up victims on Hounslow Heath. Then, however, an excessively daring attempt to rob the Parliamentarian Colonel John Hewson as he crossed the heath with a party of men resulted in the capture of Cheney and a narrow escape for John Cottington. Within days of the luckless Cheney being tried at the Old Bailey and condemned to death at Tyburn, John had found himself a new partner in crime – Captain Thomas Horne.

The captain was a much younger man than Cheney and shared some of 'Mulled Sack''s impetuosity. Although the pair carried out several successful robberies, their desire to land a really big fish proved their undoing. Or rather, the undoing of Captain Horne.

Captain Alexander Smith has described how 'Mulled Sack' seemed unable to resist the temptation of having another go at robbing Oliver Cromwell and talked his partner into accompanying him. At first all went well: the pair stopped Cromwell and his small retinue as they were going over Hounslow Heath towards Windsor, and swiftly parted the Protector from his valuables and cash. 'But', says Smith,

> a quick pursuit being made after them, a rencounter happening betwixt the highwaymen and the pursuers, the former being overpowered by numbers, Captain Horne was taken but 'Mulled Sack' had the good luck still to make his escape. The Captain

> was sent to Newgate, and receiving sentence of death at the Old Bailey, he was hanged at Tyburn.

Cottington had now lost two partners in short order, and it is perhaps not surprising that he operated on his own for the rest of his career – the highlight of which was a famous robbery at Wheatley near Oxford, when, under the startled noses of a group of soldiers, he grabbed £4,000 from an army pay-wagon. Unlike many of his contemporaries, though, John lived until the ripe old age of forty-five, finally being caught by the authorities and charged with murder and highway robbery. 'Mulled Sack' quaffed his last glass of warm sherry and went to his execution at Smithfield Rounds in April 1659.

Whether he made as good a show as his former partner, Captain Horne, is doubtful, for he certainly has no epitaph that can match this contemporary account of the handsome Cavalier's last moments:

> Captain Horne died with so much bravery and gallantry that it drew tears from many of the spectators, especially those of the female sex.

Such tears would soon be dried, however, for after the restoration of the monarchy, travellers in England were to find themselves under the threat of a new and wholly different kind of highwaymen, characterized by villainy and bloodshed. And it is with good reason that these robbers were compared to a plague …

6 A Plague of Highwaymen

The restoration of the monarchy in Britain took place in 1660 when Charles II returned from exile to his native land some nine years after the execution of his father. The king was answering the call of a distracted and impoverished nation where the fear of a revival of military despotism was growing daily. Thanks largely to the efforts of General George Monck, Charles landed at Dover and entered London in triumph on 29 May 1660.

The early years of the Restoration were to be marked by a number of dramatic changes – in particular Charles had a loyal parliament, and there was widespread support for a state and church that were both anti-Puritan and anti-Catholic. Among the ranks of the highwaymen there were to be some equally striking changes.

Not surprisingly, the return of the king brought about a dramatic fall in the number of 'Knights of the Road'. The former gentlemen Cavaliers were now able to reclaim their lands and what remained of their fortunes and were no longer driven by necessity to go a-robbing. In any event, what they had personally justified as a patriotic duty – robbing Cromwell's men – was no longer appropriate with a king on the throne.

There were, however, other men who had no such scruples and had seen what might be achieved by stalking unwary travellers. The result was a whole new generation of criminal freebooters – 'a veritable plague of highwaymen', to quote Macaulay's *History of England*.

These new highway robbers were a very different breed from the gentlemen Cavaliers and fell into two distinct categories: the organized gangs of men who co-ordinated their efforts for greater effect; and the lone operators who were almost all ruthless and sadistic men.

A traveller named Cesar de Saussure wrote at the time:

> No one caring to run the risk of being killed or maimed should argue with these highwaymen for were one to make the slightest attempt at self defence the ruffian would turn bridle and fly, but not before attempting to revenge himself by killing you. And where there are several highwaymen together, they will search you thoroughly and leave nothing.

Contemporary accounts also reveal that the highwayman's traditional method of address to a potential victim – a raised hat and a polite request for money and valuables – was now being replaced by a stream of foul-mouthed invective.

'You double-refined sons of whores!' was a frequent curse shouted from behind a pistol at a coachload of passengers. 'You suffocated dogs in doublets and sodomitical sons of bitches – hand over your cash!' There was even less respect shown to any lady travellers. 'You strumpeting whore's abortion!' a woman slow to hand over her possessions would be admonished. 'You double-poxed, long-arsed salivating bitch in grain!' And some of the expressions were even worse – the effect of the words, when spat from the mouth of a course and menacing-looking man on horseback, guaranteed to produce a speedy handing over of valuables. In some instances, even a hasty compliance with these orders might not save a woman from rape at the hands of these terrifying new brigands.

There are several interesting sources of information about this development in the history of the English highwayman, one of the most unusual being a pamphlet published in 1674, a copy of which is still in the possession of the British Museum. The title of the publication – in the typical fulsome style of the period – leaves the reader in no doubt as to the contents: *The Confession of the Four Highwaymen, as it was Written by One of Them, and Allowed by the Rest, on the 14th of this Instant April – Being the Day before their Appointed Execution*. The dog-eared and now faded little book also has a subtitle which the cynical might feel was added by the publisher to encourage sales: *This being desired to be made Publick by the Persons themselves to prevent False Reports of them when they are Dead.*

If the title-page is intriguing, the names of the four highwaymen are even more so: Francis Jackson (alias 'Dixie'), John White ('The Fowler'), John Williams ('The Matchet'), and

Walter Parkhurst who, for some reason, appears not to have enjoyed a soubriquet. The book shows all four as dyed-in-the-wool villains and there seems little doubt it was written by some hired hack, for the language in some parts almost reaches the poetical!

There is very little specific detail about the lives of these four men, beyond the fact all were Londoners and well versed in the ways of robbery and vice. A statement at the start of the narrative also declares with almost religious fervour:

> Highwaymen are devouring caterpillars of a corrupt and polluted nation. They are recruited from such that were never acquainted with an honest trade, whom either want of money or employment prompts them to undertake these dangerous designs.

And as if to drive the point home ever more fully it adds:

> All the time they can spare from robbing and undoing poor harmless men is spent on wine and women.

The four highwaymen had apparently been pursuing separate, and not entirely successful, careers in petty crime – mostly thieving and confidence tricks – when chance threw them together in a London alehouse. Jackson, who was to become the leader of the gang, was drunkenly complaining of the mistress who had just left him because he was penniless. The other three were in similarly straitened circumstances and all agreed to pool their talents and take to the highway, 'where there are fat purses to be picked'.

Uneducated though the four were, simple they certainly were not; they soon proved themselves clever strategists. It was decided that they would work in pairs: a couple would visit inns on the Maidenhead road (their choice of location) in order to pick up information on travellers; they would then join the other two to rob the appropriate coach. Thanks to tongues being loosened by drink, the partners overheard many an incautious conversation and were soon able to live in a far better style than they had enjoyed previously.

The pamphlet explains the secret of their success:

> Having made up a party, ere they proceed to act their villainies, they made a solemn vow to each other that, if by misfortune anyone should be apprehended, he shall not discover his

> accomplices; and that if he be pressed hard to particularise his companions, he must devise names for men that never were, describing their persons, features, and discovering their habitations, but so remote one from another that the danger of the trial may be over before sufficient inquiry can be made.
>
> Having taken a solemn oath to be true to one another, their next business was to acquaint themselves, by tapsters, hostlers, chamberlains, or others, what booties were stirring, how contained, and whither bound. They also had a variety of periwigs and false beards which were a good disguise and should their voices be recognised, a pebble or any suchlike thing could be put into the mouth to alter the tone.
>
> Thus provided, they fell instantly to work, riding out to rob those they had selected. And who will trust a pistol at his breast loaded with a brace of bullets and a mouth discharging at the same time a volley of oaths, that if he deliver not instantly he is a dead man?

As time passed, Jackson's gang became increasingly well known and feared – although, because of their disguises and keeping well apart from each other except when actually carrying out their robberies, little was known of their true identities. But retribution was not far away.

Francis Jackson speaks on behalf of all four when he is quoted describing how the law finally caught up with them:

> Should I enumerate all the rogueries and robberies we committed, and in what manner they were done, I should waste too much time; therefore I shall pass them all by and come to the last robbery we were guilty of near Colnbrook, when, pursued by the country, we were opposed and apprehended.

The events which lead to the gang's downfall began with an ordinary enough robbery on the road between Staines and Hounslow, which the four men had been 'working' in their usual manner for some while. However, this latest outrage seems to have finally triggered off the anger of the local population and a mounted volunteer force, armed with weapons of all sorts from muskets to pitchforks, set off in pursuit of the quartet of highwaymen.

According to the pamphlet, the gang first realized they were being followed when they reached Acton. After trading a few shots, they then rode off by way of Harrow-on-the-Hill and went, via Paddington and Kilburn, towards Hampstead Heath. Their pursuers followed relentlessly, however, forcing Jackson and his men to keep firing; and by the time the highwaymen reached the famous heath all were low on ammunition. Their horses, too, were near exhaustion – but they hoped to be safe until nightfall when they might escape under the cover of darkness.

Instead, however, a party of irregulars who had heard of the pursuit were lying in wait and, after a fierce and bloody struggle, the gang were captured. Injured, but still cursing and struggling as the sheer weight of numbers finally overpowered them, Jackson and the others were bound and then conveyed to Newgate. Within four weeks of the battle on the heath – allowing enough time for *The Confession of the Four Highwaymen* to be written down – all had been executed.

It is perhaps true to say that but for the pamphlet, the Jackson gang might well have been soon forgotten by history – particularly as there were plenty more highwaymen like them – some even worse – on the roads of England. Take the notorious twelve-strong Bracy gang who were finally brought to justice a few years later in 1679.

This group of a dozen assorted criminals is also of interest because their area of country was far away from the roads around the capital city which attracted the majority of highwaymen. Bracy and his men plagued the Midlands, in particular Derby, Newark and Nottingham. The information we have about their activities is contained in a broadsheet sold for a halfpenny in the immediate aftermath of their trial at Derby in August 1679.

Richard Bracy, the leader, was a Nottingham man with an unsavoury character. He had been imprisoned while still a child for petty theft, had apparently beaten a servant-girl to death when he was seventeen, and a year later had taken to the road as a highwayman. He was said to have been a man of fierce temper who delighted in torturing his victims, regardless of their sex. Bracy was clearly not a man to be trifled with and he ruled his gang as much by fear as his skills of leadership.

The record of the trial also provides us with the names of the other highwaymen, all also local men, though no details of their backgrounds are given. They were Richard Piggen, Roger Brookham, Joseph Gerrat, John Barker, William Loe, John

Robottom, Thomas Ouldome, John Baker, Daniel Buck, Thomas Gillat and Andrew Smedley.

The first recorded crime by the gang was actually not a highway robbery at all, but a raid on a home – though the violence of it set the pattern by which they became known. The men broke into the house of a certain John Monday at Morton, near Derby, and took away £1,200 in gold and silver, also 'binding the Esquire and all his Family in their beds and using great insolence by threats to make them confess their Treasures', according to the record of the trial.

Two months after this, the 'dirty dozen' carried out their first highway robbery on the road between Lenton and Newark where they secured several small barrels of money and packets of gold lace valued at over £1,800. They beat up the coach driver and left him seriously injured before departing to divide the proceeds.

More robberies were committed at Ockbrook, near Derby, and on the road to Everston near Nottingham, where a coach belonging to Lady Jane Scroop was apprehended. The lady was relieved of £600 but managed to thwart Bracy's attempt to rape her by slamming the coach door so sharply it caused him to fall out, the horses to bolt, and the gang leader, who had been dumped on his backside in the dust, to think twice about following her!

The gang continued their violent robberies across the Midlands for almost two years until Bracy was betrayed and disaster ensued. Unbeknownst to the other highwaymen, Bracy had previously married a woman who kept an inn near Nottingham and whom he visited from time to time in order to lie low after hold-ups. On a summer day in 1679 while Bracy lay in bed with his wife, one of the servants informed the local Justice of the Peace that a highwayman they were seeking was in the house. The inn was surrounded and after a brief exchange of gunfire, Bracy was taken into custody.

Despite losing their leader, the remaining members of the gang decided to continue robbing travellers – but one disaster followed another and within a matter of three months all had been captured. Two of the men, Richard Piggen and John Baker, turned King's evidence, and the subsequent trial became a formality. During the hearing, any sympathy there might have been for the Bracy gang disappeared when it was revealed how a young pot-boy of fifteen had accidentally overheard some of their plans and, despite his tearful pleas for mercy, had been cold-bloodedly murdered and buried in a cellar.

Another gang of highwaymen who operated at this period chose the road to Newmarket as their hunting-ground – and with good reason, for since the days of James I the East Anglian town had attracted great numbers of wealthy men and women to the horse-races which were regularly held there. Members of the court of the new king, Charles II, rubbed shoulders with gamblers of all kinds, carrying their bulging purses to Newmarket in the hope of increasing their fortunes.

Waiting for these sportsmen was the self-styled 'Captain' Tom Gray and his gang of four. He was a handsome-looking but depraved and cruel man, apparently as adept at lifting a skirt as he was a purse; it is said he took restitution from impoverished victims by ravishing the women in any group while the members of his gang looked on admiringly.

Charles Harper has provided further detail about the Newmarket road in an account of five highwaymen who, though he does not name them, were in all probability 'Captain' Gray's men.

> As the fame and vogue of Newmarket increased, so also did the highway robberies on the Newmarket Road. The culminating point of all appears to have been a pitched battle which, according to the *Domestic Intelligence* of August 24, 1680, took place at the Devil's ditch, through which the highway runs on to Newmarket Heath. Five highwaymen had here robbed a coach and taken £50 and a very considerable booty in the way of gold lace, silks and linen. Before they could make off with the plunder, the exasperated countryfolk were roused and were stationed in a body in the opening of that tall and steep bank, impracticable for horsemen, the only way by which the Heath may be entered or left.
>
> The highwaymen were thus completely shut in and could only escape by abandoning their horses, an unthinkable alternative. Had they retreated, they would have been captured in Newmarket town. The only thing to be done was to make a dash for liberty. 'Knowing themselves Dead Men by the Law, if they were taken,' says that early newspaper, 'they charged through the countrymen, and by firing upon them wounded four, one of which we understand is dead of his wounds.' Thus they got clear

away: the whole incident leaving upon the mind a very vivid impression of a lawless and ill-policed country.

Other newspapers of this period provide further evidence about the gangs of highwaymen spreading like a rash across the countryside. Interestingly, some of those who lost their valuables began to offer rewards for the capture of their assailants, as illustrated by the following report which appeared in the pages of the *London Gazette* of 1 December 1681.

ROBBED the 10th of November last from Mr. Joseph Bullock of Bristol on the road between Hungerford and Newbury in Berkshire, one Silver Watch and Case, there being on the backside of the Case an Almanac, a Hanger with a Plate hilt, and a Buff Belt with Silver Buckles.

The advertiser also provided a handy description of his assailants:

There were three men, the one a middle-sized man, full faced with a short white wig much curled, in an old cloth-coloured riding coat on a flea-bitten horse, about 14 hands high, his brows brown; the second man a middle-sized black favoured man, with black hair or wig and thin favour, on a grey horse above 14 hands high; and the third a full grown man, thin favoured with curled dark brown hair. Whoever can discover the Persons aforesaid to Mr. Bullock of Bristol, or at the 'Three Cups' in Bread Street, London (the said Robbers having killed one John Thomas, the said Mr. Bullock's servant) shall have their Charges and £10 reward.

Three years on very little had changed, for the *London Gazette* was again giving column inches to details of an equally violent attack on another traveller who was similarly offering a reward for information. The location of this robbery will doubtless be familiar to most readers.

On Whit Sunday in the evening was committed a great Robbery by four Highwaymen within half a mile of Watford Gap to the value of about £800 taken from some four passengers. The men were of indifferent features, their coats were all turned up with shag, one had a blue shag, and wore a Perriwig, the others wore their own hair. They had two bay nags, a bay mare somewhat

> battered before, and a sprig tail Sorrel Mare, which they took away from one they robbed, and a black nag. One of them had short holsters to his saddle without breast-plate, another a pair of pistols in his saddle cover. Whoever gives notice of the said Robbers to Joshuah Snowden, Confectioner at the Belsavage Gate on Ludgate Hill, or to Henry Keys at Watford Gap Inn, shall be rewarded.

Other newspapers in the closing decade of the seventeenth century tell similar stories. On 9 November, 1690 on the road to St Albans, for instance, a gang of seven highwaymen carried out an audacious robbery on the Manchester carrier which was taking some £15,000 in tax money to London and was being guarded by what was described as a 'strong' escort. These desperadoes carried out their hold-up with amazing cool, waylaying the party, overpowering the escort with only a minimum use of weapons, and, after grabbing the money, disappearing without trace. In order to frustrate any attempts at pursuit, the highwaymen cold-bloodedly killed or hamstrung the guards' eighteen horses.

It may well have been this same gang who carried out another dare-devil raid in November 1692 when they stopped a party of fifteen butchers on their way to buy cattle at Thame market in Oxfordshire. The unfortunate traders were stripped of their cash and valuables, worth in excess of £10,000, and left bound and gagged in a ditch until they were discovered by other passers-by later in the day.

Perhaps, though, the most extraordinary gang of highwaymen at this time was the thirty-strong force who boldly set up a headquarters in Epping Forest and, day and night, robbed travellers on the roads to Cambridge and Newmarket. A report written in 1698 declares:

> They did not hesitate to slay, and often the bodies of slaughtered wayfarers affrighted the next travellers, who, warned by such sights of the futility of resistance, rendered unto these Highway Caesars whatever they had upon them: satisfied to escape, with empty pockets indeed, but with a whole skin. For a while this settlement of reckless men was abolished by a raid, under the direction of the Lord Chief Justice, but the expedition, raiding in the interests of law and order, had not long departed when the highwaymen again occupied the spot. They even had the impudence to send a written and signed defiance to Whitehall.

At this show of arrogance, a second force was dispatched to Epping Forest and this time the law managed to capture or disperse the thirty 'Highway Caesars' once and for all.

Not all highwaymen during this time worked in groups – there were still the loners, men of cruel nerve and usually of unsavoury morals, some of whom enjoyed almost as much success as the gangs. A trio of them must suffice to represent the brotherhood as a whole.

Typical of such men was Jacob Halsey, a Bedfordshire farmer's son who was raised as a Quaker but fell into bad company and, after a period of petty thieving, sensed there were richer pickings on the road and so became a highwayman. He disguised himself in a periwig and long coat and on the road between Barnet and St Albans took sixty pounds from his first victim, an aged money-lender from Bedford. Before departing from the scene of his crime, Halsey shot the man's horse and left his victim tied to a tree with the rope cruelly tight around his neck.

In the months which followed he committed several robberies on the road between Abingdon and Oxford. But when one of his victims proved to be only carrying fourteen shillings, the enraged Halsey beat him senseless, tore off his clothes, and nailed the man's foreskin to a tree, according to Captain Alexander Smith.

The historian of highwaymen relates another grim example of Halsey's sense of humour which occurred after he had held up a very pretty young woman he encountered on horseback travelling on the road from Maningtree towards Harwich in Essex.

> The conveniency of the place giving him encouragement to be carnally-minded, Halsey said to the gentlewomen, 'My pretty lamb, an insurrection of an unruly member obliges me to make use of you upon an extraordinary occasion, therefore I must dismount thy alluring body, to the end that I may come into thee.' Accordingly he brought the gentlewoman unto a bye road, where fastening her horses to a tree, he took her into an adjacent cornfield, where the lofty product of Ceres hid his lascivious embraces; and having surfeited himself with unlawful pleasure, he sent her about her business, without so much as searching her pockets or taking the gold watch which she had then by her side.

Halsey did not always allow his female victims to keep their valuables, however – whether they had pleased him or not – and stories of his outrages soon made him dreaded throughout the southern counties. When, though, he overreached himself and attempted to rob the powerful Earl of Westmorland near his estate at Wateringbury in Kent, Halsey was overpowered and committed to Maidstone Gaol. Here a recital of his misdeeds condemned him to death in April 1691.

In a final speech he could not resist a last boast about his sexual prowess, declaring, 'I have robbed many people, but never killed a man or woman. I tried many of the fair sex, and let me tell ye 'tis a pleasant sin to play with them, let their religion be what it will. Ah! brethren, that stubborn piece of flesh has no forecast at all!'

Thomas Wilmot, another lone adventurer who was hanged the following year, treated women with even more brutality. Born in Ipswich, Suffolk, the son of a wealthy squire, Wilmot squandered his inheritance of £600 on high living and fast women, and then took to the roads. For a while he made his hauls along the road between Colchester and Chelmsford; he then moved to another stretch which ran from Dorking in Surrey to Petworth in Sussex, before the hue and cry he raised forced him to move to the west of England.

Amongst Wilmot's victims at this time was a lady who, he was angry to find, had only eight pounds in silver coins on her. Spotting a large diamond ring on her finger, the highwayman ordered her to take it off. But as she struggled to remove it, claims a report, Wilmot grew impatient and 'such was his barbarity that he cut off the finger with a knife, swearing at the same time that since he was compelled to live by robbing through his once great fondness of the fair sex he was resolved in all his robberies to show a woman the least favour'.

Such, indeed, was Wilmot's cruelty that, after a narrow escape from capture in Kent, he fled from the country to Europe. There he added murder to his crimes by slaughtering a Swiss couple, their three children and a serving maid, when they discovered him robbing their home. On his return to England, he was finally apprehended while robbing the Duke of Buckingham in Northamptonshire and, following a short trial, was hanged in May 1692, aged thirty-eight.

Patrick O'Bryan, the last of our trio, was an equally

bloodthirsty villain who once boasted of having cut up the body of one of his highway victims with a sword. O'Bryan, who was born into an impoverished Irish family at Loughrea in Galway, came over to England after Charles II had returned, and there joined the Coldstream Guards. But being addicted to vice, and running up heavy gambling debts with the other guards, he was soon forced to desert and took to the high road.

A robbery at Hackney first brought O'Bryan to the public notice when he took all the money and jewellery from a couple and then left the pair, a poet named D'Urffey and his lover, Mrs Needham, stark naked in a field! A second escapade guaranteed his reputation – for this time his victim was none other than the royal favourite, Nell Gwynne, whose coach he stopped on the road to Winchester. His address to the king's mistress is now a matter of record:

> Madam, I am a gentleman, and, as you see, a very able one. I have done a great many signal services to the fair sex, and have, in return, been all my life maintained by them. Now, as I know you to be a charitable whore, I make bold to ask you for a little money: though I never had the honour of serving you in particular. However, if any opportunity shall ever fall in my way, you may depend upon it I will exert myself to the utmost for I scorn to be ungrateful!

There was a code of honour, it would seem, between whores and highwaymen, for Nell handed over the ten guineas she was carrying, with a smile; and O'Bryan allowed her to go on her way without laying a hand upon her. He did not treat another of his female victims so generously, however.

In 1687 at Trowbridge in Wiltshire, O'Bryan robbed a Mr Lancelot Wilmot and his family of £2,500 in gold and silver. He was so captivated by the unhappy man's daughter that, as he was about to leave, he suddenly declared, 'Before I tie and gag this pretty creature I must make bold to rob her of her maidenhead.'

The girl, however, put up a spirited resistance before O'Bryan was finally able to ravish her. Then, having satisfied his lust, he stabbed the girl and murdered both her mother and father. Only a servant escaped to report this appalling slaughter.

In fact another two years were to pass before O'Bryan's bloody career was brought to an end, when he was arrested while trying to commit a robbery at the Haymarket in London.

As soon as his identity was discovered, he was hustled smartly off to Salisbury to stand trial for the murders at Trowbridge. The Irishman was executed in April 1689, with not a soul to shed a tear at his passing.

It would be wrong, however, to imagine that *all* highwaymen during the reign of Charles II were either sadistic loners or the members of murderous gangs. For there were exceptions whose characters and exploits have lifted them far above the rank and file of highway robbers so that they have become, in effect, the superstars of the road. Men like William Davis (nick-named the 'Golden Farmer'), Thomas Sympson (known, curiously, as 'Old Mob'), John Nevison (called 'Swift Nicks'), and, perhaps most famous of all, the dashing 'Squire of Dames', Claude Duval ...

7 England's Greatest Highwayman Was French!

Until about 150 years ago, the remains of a famous highwayman's house stood on the Hornsey Road near where it joins Holloway Road at the busy London junction known as Seven Sisters. Referred to by generations of people as 'The Devil's House', it had originally been a moated timber building, Old Tollington House, which became the manor house of Highbury, until it was converted into a tavern for the sale of beer and spirits.

The house, standing just two fields away from the Holloway turnpike – and today within walking distance of the famous Arsenal football stadium – was believed to have been the favourite retreat of Claude Duval, 'The Squire of Dames', the most gallant and dashing of all seventeenth century highwaymen, during the years when he held up coaches and seduced lady travellers on the northern approaches to London. Such, indeed, was this man's fame that, after his execution, what is now Hornsey Road was, for a time, known as Duval's Lane – though there are some older maps which give the original name as 'Devil's Lane'.

No matter which is true, the fame of Duval has survived both the disappearance of the remains of that mansion turned public house in around 1849, and the many and varied interpretations of his exploits. It is perhaps no wonder that a legend should have grown up about this man, for fiction became mixed with fact very early on. Vide this remark in Captain Alexander Smith's biography written less than fifty years after Duval's death:

> Of all the highwaymen who have been executed within the limits of Great Britain, none have been more noted than Claude Du Vall [one of several variant spellings of his name], who, as some

> say, was born in Smock Alley, without Bishopsgate, though, indeed he received his birth at a place called Domfront in Normandy, France.

Although some historians of this period subscribed in the past to the theory that Duval *was* English, research has subsequently established beyond all reasonable doubt that the best-known English highwayman of the seventeenth century was actually French. With hindsight, he appears to have been a truly grandiloquent figure – Leigh Hunt, for example, in the *Indicator*, refers to him as 'an eternal feather in the cap of highway gentility'. While there was, certainly, much to separate him from the cut-throats of the last chapter, he was also a man with an immoral, and occasionally ruthless, streak in him. Duval may well have been loved by many ladies but – perhaps *because* – he treated them rough.

The real facts of his life can, though, be distilled from various accounts, beginning with the allegedly autobiographical *Memoirs of Monsieur Du Vall* (published only a few days after his execution in 1670) – with its delightful subheading: *Intended as a severe reflection on the too great fondness of English ladies towards French footmen which at that time of day was a too common complaint*. A copy of this survives in the British Museum, where its authorship has been attributed to one William Page, MD. Then there are the essays in such major works of reference as Macaulay's *History of England* (where Duval is one of only two highwaymen to be accorded a mention by name) and the *Dictionary of National Biography*, which notes of his fame that it 'rested hardly less on his gallantry to ladies than on his daring robberies'. Nor can the accounts of Captain Alexander Smith and Charles Harper be overlooked. The latter, though highly sceptical of some of the surely apocryphal stories told about our man, has still declared:

> Claude Du Val ranks among his brother highwaymen as high as Rembrandt or Raphael among artists. He was, indeed, no less an artist in his own profession than they. He might not, and probably did not, acquire as much of other people's property as did Captain Hind, but artists are not necessarily moneymakers.

The first myth that can be dismissed about Duval is that he was born in England. There is proof he was born in 1643 in the town of Domfront in Normandy, the son of a respectable miller, Pierre Du Vall, and his wife, Marguerite; his entry into England was as part of the entourage of Charles II. For just as the exiled king was planning a new life, so the handsome and clever Duval hoped a change of scenery would open new horizons for him. Initially, though, he had not planned on becoming a highway robber.

Young Claude received a sound, if basic, education which qualified him as a footman. An apocryphal story from his childhood says that a fortune-teller who visited Domfront saw a mark like two crowns on the boy's forehead which, he said, indicated he would be a traveller, never without money and always in favour with women. Accurate the prediction may have been, but Duval certainly had no such mark upon him.

At fourteen, the boy was urged to leave home and seek his fortune. He is next heard of in Paris where he was 'a little given to filching', but managed to secure a job as a page in the service of the Duke of Richmond, one of the group of exiles waiting to return to England under the Restoration. (It has been alleged that the Duchess of Richmond was instrumental in the dark-eyed young man being taken into her husband's service and that he was for a time her lover.) At the age of seventeen, Duval landed in England, where his alert mind spotted that there were better spoils to be had robbing wealthy travellers than being a page-boy or even doing 'a little filching'.

A broadsheet, colourfully describing his early days as a highwayman, states:

> With the defeat of Puritanism, smart carriages again clattered through the dark, jewels flashed in the moonlight, and highwaymen flocked to the roads. Duval joined them, tempted by the easy money. With morals easier, he spent his spare time courting ladies of fashion. The handsome young Frenchman was conspicuously successful in both pursuits.

The impact Duval made was soon evident in print when the *London Gazette* placed him at the head of a list of wanted highwaymen; while, if we can believe contemporary gossip, his silver tongue and charming manners enabled him to take possession of his female victims' bodies as well as their valuables. The accounts also state that although he usually robbed on his own, he was occasionally assisted by some admiring English accomplices.

Hampstead Heath became one of Duval's favourite locations, and it was here in about 1668 that an event occurred which was to make him celebrated not only in society conversation, but also in the press, in song, poetry and art. As the encounter has been much paraphrased, it is worth quoting the original version from the *Memoirs* in full.

> He, with his Squadron, overtakes a Coach, which they had set up over night, having intelligence of a booty of £400 in it. In the coach was a knight, his lady, and only one serving maid, who, perceiving five horsemen making up to them, presently imagined that they were beset; and they were confirmed in this apprehension by seeing them whisper to one another, and ride backwards and forwards. The lady, to shew that she was not afraid, takes a Flageolet out of her pocket and plays. Du Vall takes the hint, plays also, and excellently well, upon a Flageolet of his own, and in this posture he rides up to the coach side.
>
> 'Sir,' says he to the person in the coach, 'your lady plays excellently and I doubt not but that she dances as well. Will you please to walk out of the coach and let me have the honour to dance one coranto with her upon the heath?' 'Sir,' said the person in the coach, 'I dare not deny anything to one of your quality and good mind. You seem a gentleman and your request is very reasonable.'
>
> Which said, the footman opens the door, out comes the knight, Du Vall leaps lightly off his horse and hands the lady out of the coach. They danced, and here it was that Du Vall performed marvels: the best masters in London except those that are French, not being able to show such footing as he did in his great French riding boots. The dancing being over (there being no violins, Du Vall sung the coranto himself) he waits on the lady to her coach. As the knight was going in, says Du Vall to him, 'Sir, you have forgot to pay for the music.' 'No, I have not,' replied the knight, and, putting his hand under the seat of the coach, pulls out £100 in a bag and delivers it to him, which Du Vall took with a very good grace, and courteously answered, 'Sir, you are liberal, and shall have no cause to repent your being so; this liberality of yours shall excuse you the other £300,' and giving the word that if he met with any more of the crew, he might pass undisturbed, he civilly takes his leave of him.

The story of this extraordinary hold-up became the talk of

Founders of the highway tradition: the 'Mother' of highwaywomen, Moll Cutpurse (*above*) and the 'Father', Robin Hood (*below*)

James Maclaine, the darling of the ladies, at whose trial (*below*) several ladies pleaded for his life

The curiously named 'Mulled Sack' carrying out one of his most successful robberies – taking over £4,000 from the Oxford Wagon

A gang of highwaymen waiting for a coach

'The Biter Bit' – a highwayman finds himself the prisoner of the travellers he has just robbed

Jackſon's Recantation

OR, THE

LIFE & DEATH

OF THE

NOTORIOUS HIGH-WAY-MAN

NOW

HANGING in CHAINS

AT

HAMPSTEAD

DELIVERED

To a Friend, a little before Execution; Wherein
is truly diſcovered the whole Myſtery of
that Wicked and Fatal Profeſſion
Of PADDING on the ROAD

LONDON,

Printed for I. B. in the Year 1674

Title-page of the highwayman Francis Jackson's famous Recantation, published in 1674

The dashing highwayman, Claude Duval, performing his famous dance on Hounslow Heath

'The Golden Farmer', William Davis, who led a remarkable double life as gentleman farmer and highway robber

A contemporary engraving of Turpin in his hideout in Epping Forest

The real Dick Turpin – the sadistic bully putting an old woman on the fire to make her reveal the whereabouts of her money

London, and the handsome French highwayman was soon such a favourite that even modern stars of the entertainment world might envy him. 'Maids, widows and wives, the rich, the poor, the noble, the vulgar, all submitted to him,' says another report of the time. But Duval was not always in such a good humour, and on one occasion on Blackheath he certainly blotted his copybook not only in the eyes of his admirers but also those of one of his men.

On the heath he and the others held up a coach which turned out to contain several ladies, including one who was giving her child some milk from a silver feeding-bottle. Whether Duval was desperately in need of money at that time there is no way of knowing, but, apart from taking all the ladies' valuables, he also insisted on the child's feeding-bottle. As this was taken, the child began to scream.

According to virtually all accounts of this episode, it was one of Duval's accomplices who demanded the bottle, and the Frenchman, on hearing the screams and seeing what had happened, who insisted that it was given back. However, in the *Memoirs* it is stated quite categorically that Duval demanded the bottle and it was one of the accomplices who had the courage to tell *him* to return it!

Such a story could well have been regarded by later writers who had a vested interest in portraying him favourably, as taking some of the gloss off the Duval legend: hence the reversal of roles in most subsequent accounts. It also has to be reported that Duval's final capture was not the dramatic cornering of a brave adventurer these same authorities would have us believe.

Duval's career continued for another two years, including robberies in Hounslow, Oxford, and Windsor Forest (where he took fifty pounds from Squire Roper, master of the king's hounds, sending him home roped by his neck and heels to his horse); followed by a brief return to his native France, where he boasted of his success with English gentlemen's purses (and their ladies' honours) to admiring Parisians.

Shortage of money, however, drew Duval back to London, and, after a modest snatch on the outskirts of the city, he carelessly got drunk at an inn called the Hole in the Wall in Chandos Street, Covent Garden, and was arrested. In his befuddled state, the dashing highwayman was unable to draw either his sword or pistols before he was clapped in Newgate.

He was thereafter speedily arraigned, convicted and sentenced to death at Tyburn on 21 January 1670. England's most famous French highwayman was just twenty-seven years old when he died.

Duval's last hours were at least spent in the style to which he was accustomed, for, according to Captain Alexander Smith:

> There were a great company of ladies and those not of the meanest degree that visited him in prison, interceded for his pardon, and accompanied him to the gallows, with swollen eyes and cheeks blubbered with tears under their vizards.

Even when the hangman had done his work, Duval was not allowed to lie still.

> After he had hanged a convenient time, he was cut down, and by persons well dressed, carried into a mourning coach, and so conveyed to the Tangier Tavern in St. Giles's where he lay in state all that night, the room hung with black cloth, the hearse covered with scutcheons, eight wax tapers burning, as many tall gentlemen with long cloaks attending. Mum was the word, and great silence expected from all that visited, for fearing of disturbing this sleeping lion.

According to several reports published after Duval's death, strenuous efforts had been made by friends in high places to have the highwaymen freed – though who they were, male or female, is not stated – and it has been said that Charles II would have pardoned him on account of his gratitude to France, but Judge Morton, the trial judge and one of the most respected justices in the country, threatened to resign if this happened. Such stories merely added to Duval's growing legend, which pamphleteers did much to promote with wholly imaginary stories of his amatory conquests – ranging from the seduction of a 13-year-old girl to win a bet, and of a 60-year-old woman to cuckold her pompous husband. A spurious 'last speech' allegedly found on Duval's body after he had been hanged, in which he thanked the ladies of England for their favours, was also published and sold countless thousands of copies. (This 'dying confession' which some later authors have further claimed that Duval actually read before being hanged at Tyburn, is reprinted in the appendix to this book.)

Duval was buried in St Paul's Church, Covent Garden, after a splendid funeral – 'attended by a numerous train of mourners, most whereof were of the beautiful sex', says one contemporary account. His body was placed under a white marble stone complete with a coat of arms (to which he was not entitled) and a suitable epitaph. Although this was destroyed when the original church was burned down in 1759, a scribe had fortunately taken down the words, which still survive:

> Here lies Du Vall: Reader, if Male thou art,
> Look to they purse; if Female to thy heart.
> Much havoc has he made of both; for all
> Men he made stand, and women he made fall.
> The second Conqueror of the Norman race,
> Knights to his arms did yield, and Ladies to his face.
> Old Tyburn's Glory; England's illustrious thief,
> Du Vall, the Ladies' joy; Du Vall, the Ladies' grief.

There is a building still in existence which forms a permanent reminder of the second remarkable seventeenth century highwayman, William Davis, the colourfully named 'Golden Farmer'. The building, a public house in Surrey called the Jolly Farmer is to be found just to the west of Bagshot at the junction of the roads to Camberley and Frimley. Previously known as the Golden Farmer, its sign commemorated the achievements of the local man who not only carried out his robberies for what is, most likely, the longest career of any highwayman – over forty years – but was so cunning at disguising his identity that not even his wife and family – and there were eighteen children in all – had the slightest idea about his other life, until he was finally caught.

The reasons for William Davis becoming a highwayman have been much debated. He was a farmer by profession, and cultivated a sizeable piece of land on the edge of Bagshot Heath. He had married well and proceeded to raise his large family, giving the impression to all the world of being a hard worker and a devoted father. If he had an eccentricity, said local people, it was his habit of paying all his bills with gold. No paper money was ever seen to be handled by him – and it was this practice which earned him the nickname the Golden Farmer among his friends and creditors.

So why did Davis take to the road? Was it, as some have said, because of that enormous brood and the difficulty of providing for them on what was regarded as inferior agricultural land? Or was it, as others have argued, because he could not resist the lure of Bagshot Heath, then regarded as one of the most profitable of highwaymen's haunts? And how, everyone has asked, did he allay the suspicions of his family and hired helpers about his absences from the farm, and avoid having to explain settling his debts with what appeared to be an inexhaustible supply of gold coins?

But, since Davis preserved his secret to the end, the real answer will probably never be known. What is certain, though, is that he was a master of disguise, for he made a speciality of daylight robberies at a time when most of his confederates preferred the cover of night. And, whilst the baffled authorities sought this elusive will-o'-the-wisp, Davis himself grew in public esteem as a pillar of the local church and a generous benefactor of charities.

The 'Golden Farmer' was actually Welsh, having been born in Wrexham, Denbighshire, in 1627. In his teens his family moved to Gloucestershire and it was here that he met the daughter of a wealthy innkeeper and married her. When Davis's father-in-law helped him to lease a farm near Bagshot for his rapidly increasing family, he seemed, to all intents and purposes, firmly on the road to a comfortable, if hard-working, life. Quite when he first put on a disguise, saddled one of his horses and slipped away to begin preying on unsuspecting travellers – in particular stock-breeders and farmers like himself – has never been accurately determined, and is all the more difficult to determine because he rarely worked other than on his own. It seems probable, however, that he made his debut shortly before 1650, while still in his early twenties.

The lurid pamphlets published after his capture mostly contradict one another about the number and type of his robberies – but there are a few which unmistakably bear the signs of his handiwork. His initial sorties were mostly against local stock-drovers on their return from market with the proceeds of their sales – though on one occasion he demonstrated a nice sense of impudence by robbing his own landlord after the man had called to collect the annual rent of seventy guineas.

Secretly arming himself after the landlord had left the farm,

Davis galloped after the man and confronted him on the road. When the hapless fellow argued he had only a few shillings upon him, Davis wagged a pistol at him and told him to empty his purse. Within minutes he was once again in possession of his gold. And when the landlord made a return visit to Bagshot, so the story goes, he found a most sympathetic listener to his tale in William Davis!

Captain Alexander Smith relates another amusing exploit from the early years of the 'Golden Farmer's' career, when he had started to roam further afield in search of victims.

> One Mr. Hart, a young gentleman of Enfield, who had a good estate but not overmuch wit, and therefore could sooner change a piece of gold than a piece of sense, riding over Finchley Common, where the Golden Farmer had been hunting about four or five hours for a prey, he rides up to him, and giving the gentleman a slap over his shoulder with the flat of his drawn hanger, quoth he, 'A plague on you, how slow you are, to make a man wait on you all this morning; come deliver what you have, and be poxed to you, and then go to hell for orders.'
>
> The gentleman, who was wont to find a more agreeable entertainment betwixt his mistress and his snuff-box, being surprised at this rustical sort of greeting, began to make several excuses, and say he had no money about him; but his antagonist not believing him, he made bold to search his pockets himself, and finding in them above a hundred guineas, besides a gold watch, he gave him two or three good slaps over his shoulder again, with his hanger, and at the same time bade him not to give his mind to lying any more when an honest gentleman required a small boon of him.

Apart from his sense of humour, the 'Golden Farmer' possessed a sharp tongue which he used freely against any man – or woman – who defied his call to hand over their valuables. A typical instance of this occurred when he was as far from home as Salisbury Plain and came across a coach containing the Duchess of Albemarle. The duchess was, however, well protected by a coachman, postilion and two footmen, but they seemingly had little stomach for a fight with the lone highwayman, for reports claim that he injured all four without suffering so much as a scratch himself.

Even after watching this fracas, the lady in the carriage still refused to hand over her valuables to Davis. His temper rising, without any more ado, the 'Golden Farmer' snatched a gold watch from her side, three diamond rings from her fingers, and bawled at her: 'You bitch incarnate, you would rather look at your face in the glass every morning than give an honest man a small matter to support him in his lawful occasions on the road!'

Those who read about this robbery at the time probably allowed themselves a wry smile – for the duchess was no demure lady unused to such language. Before her marriage she had been plain Nan Clarges, the daughter of a blacksmith, whom Samuel Pepys had referred to in his diary as 'Dirty Bess', and who kept an appallingly ill-run household and had once served him bad meat at a dinner.

Another coach-load of five gentlewomen whom Davis also held up in the Salisbury area similarly got the rough edge of his tongue when one of their number, a Quaker, refused to hand over her jewellery. After remonstrating politely with the woman, he suddenly took her by the shoulder – one of his later chroniclers states – and 'shaking her like as a mastiff does a bull', he shouted:

> You canting bitch! If you dally with me at this rate, you'll certainly provoke my spirit to be damnable rude to you! You see these good women here who were so tender-hearted as to be charitable to me, and you, you whining whore, are so covetous as to lose your life for the sake of mammon. Come, come you hollow-hearted bitch, unpin your purse-strings quickly, or else I shall send you out of the land of the living.

With the highwayman's masked face just inches from hers and feeling his hot breath on her cheek, the lady swiftly complied, handing over a purse of fifty guineas, a gold watch and a diamond ring. After that, concludes the report, 'they parted then as good friends as if they'd never fallen out at all!'

Once more the 'Golden Farmer' rode off into the distance … to reappear, apparently unmissed, as farmer Davis of Bagshot, where he continued his rural pursuits until the call of the road drew him again.

During his career, Davis robbed a number of well-known people including Sir Thomas Day, a Justice of the Peace, from whom he took sixty pounds in gold coins on the road between Gloucester and Worcester; and Squire Broughton, a barrister of the Middle Temple, whom he relieved of thirty guineas, eleven pieces of gold, some silver and a gold watch at Hillingdon on the road into London. According to reports, the 'Golden Farmer' changed his clothing to suit his victims, and his disguises ranged from those of a simple rustic to a gentleman of means.

For some forty years, William Davis pursued this extraordinary double life, seeing his children grow to maturity and leave home without the faintest idea that their father was one of the country's most wanted highwaymen. When fate finally caught up with him it was very close to home – caused by a surprising error for a man of such experience, although he was then in his sixties.

He had just robbed a coach on the Exeter road near Bagshot Heath and was turning to ride away, when one of his victims pulled a pistol from underneath a seat and shot the departing figure in the back. Davis tumbled from his horse and lay still as two gentlemen from the coach nervously approached him. When they rolled the highwayman over and pulled off his mask a first-class sensation ensued.

The revelation of the identity of the 'Golden Farmer' as a respected local farmer became the talk of the country and the subject of lengthy newspaper reports after the man himself confessed. His wife was dumbstruck, his sons unbelieving, and his daughters mortified, as several had already married with dowries that had obviously been provided by his nefarious activities. An extraordinary double life came to an end when William Davis was committed to Newgate, and, after trial, executed on 20 December 1689. He was sixty-four years old.

To add to the shame the Davis family had already suffered – and as a warning to others – the body of the 'Golden Farmer' was taken back to Bagshot Heath and there hung in chains until nothing remained but the bare bones of his skeleton.

The only other highwayman that Davis is known to have occasionally worked with is the curiously named 'Old Mob', a.k.a. Thomas Sympson, whose legend also looms large in the history of the seventeenth century. Although both men preferred operating alone, there is evidence that they hunted together about half a dozen times and admired each other's bravado and wit. Both enjoyed careers of much the same duration, although with the absence of precise dates for Sympson it is impossible to state whether his was the longer.

Sympson was born in Romsey, Hampshire, at some date in

the first part of the century. Little is known of his family or of his sparse education, and still less about how he came by his nickname. Indeed, Sympson seems to have cloaked his life in the same kind of secrecy as his erstwhile companion in crime – and like Davis he lived in one place, his native Romsey, marrying and raising five children, who in turn had children of their own, before he was finally brought to justice. Despite the success he was to enjoy during a career which ranged across the south and west of England, 'Old Mob' seems in hindsight much less of a character than either Davis or Duval. He was, in essence, an accomplished highwayman who robbed efficiently, had a ready reply when challenged, and remained one step ahead of the law for far longer than virtually anyone else of his kind.

The records of 'Old Mob's' crimes indicate that he aimed high: not for him mere farmers and stock-drovers, but knights of the realm and their ladies. One of his earliest hold-ups was of a certain Sir Bartholomew Shower on the road between Honiton and Exeter, an event which revealed his cool nerve. Finding that his victim had very little money on him, Sympson ordered the man to draw a bill for £150 which, after it had been written and Sir Bartholomew secured to a tree, the highwayman rode off to Exeter to cash. He did have the grace, though, to return after successfully negotiating the bill and free the enraged knight!

Sympson showed similar nerve when he found the man facing his pistol in another coach was none other than George Jeffreys, then the Lord Chief Justice of England, well known for the harshness of his sentences. In Smith's version, when Judge Jeffreys began to prevaricate, Sympson proved that he, too, was a man of words.

> I don't doubt that when justice has overtaken us both, I shall stand at least as good a chance as your lordship, who have already written your name in indelible characters of blood by putting to death so many hundred innocent men, for only standing up in defence of our common liberties, that you might secure the favour of your prince. 'Tis enough for you to preach morality upon the Bench, when nobody dares to contradict you; but your lessons can have no effect upon me at this time.

Judge Jeffreys had no alternative but to hand over the fifty-six guineas in his purse.

Another victim who received a similar riposte from 'Old Mob' was the Duchess of Portsmouth whose retinue he halted on the road from Newmarket. The duchess was perhaps better known as the Frenchwoman, Louise de Kerouaille, one of Charles II's mistresses, who had been enobled for her 'services'. A beautiful but haughty woman, she immediately challenged the highwayman, as Captain Alexander Smith has reported:

> 'Do you know who you stop?' quoth her Grace. 'Yes, madam,' replied Old Mob, 'I know you to be the greatest whore in the kingdom, and that you are maintained at the public charge. I know that all the courtiers depend upon your smiles, and even the King is your slave. But a gentleman-collector upon the road is a greater man, and more absolute, than His Majesty is at Court. Therefore I must presume to take what you have, without asking any more questions.'
>
> The Duchess at these words, being very angry, she upbraided him with his impudence, and told him flat and plain, she would not part with what she had, nay furthermore, she bid him touch her if he durst. 'Indeed,' quoth Old Mob, 'I durst if I die for it; therefore you outlandish bitch, deliver; for as you have no commodity about you but what is French, I may answer, by law, the seizure of that prohibited by an Act of Parliament.' So beginning to fall on board her in a very boisterous manner, her Grace quickly cried out for quarter, which Old Mob quickly gave, upon surrendering £200 in money which was in her coach, beside a rich necklace, a gold watch and some diamond rings.

Undoubtedly, though, Thomas Sympson's most famous highway robbery was the one he committed dressed in women's clothing! While staying in Bath he learned of a certain wealthy lord (whose identity is unfortunately not disclosed in any of the contemporary reports) who was about to return to London. The man was a reknowned lecher, and 'Old Mob' decided to have some amusement at the man's expense: both physically and financially.

Charmingly disguised in a flowing skirt and cloak, with 'her' face hidden behind a veil, Sympson rode up alongside the nobleman's coach and was soon engaged in conversation. After a while, says a later account, 'his lordship being amorously inclined, he was for fulfilling the primary command – increase and multiply.' For 'Old Mob', though, there was the little matter of the man's six attendants – but at a flutter of 'her' eyelids, and the promise of complying with the request as long as it was in a place of privacy, the old lecher succumbed.

The six attendents who knew their master's lusts of old, thought no more of it as he rode off with his 'pretty doxy' into a convenient wood. The report then continues: 'Alighting with an intention of enjoyment in the folds of love, his lordship, for an introduction to the font of pleasure, was now for taking up the petticoats.'

One can imagine his surprise when he discovered not a petticoat but a man's breeches and, on enquiring why 'she' was wearing them, being told by 'Old Mob' as he threw back his veil and pulled out a pistol, 'Why, my lord, to put your money in!' And having bound the old roué hand and foot, Sympson was able to ride off with over £150 worth of valuables.

Such exploits naturally made Thomas Sympson a favourite with the pamphleteers when he was finally caught in London in 1691. He faced a total of thirty-six charges of highway robbery and went to the gallows at Tyburn on 12 September, a smile still on his ageing features. Among those who watched his end were two of his children and several tearful grandchildren – making him the only known person among the notoriously short-lived band of highwaymen ever to have attained the distinction of becoming a grandfather.

The last of the quartet of great seventeenth century robbers was John Nevison, known to many as 'Swift Nicks', a man deserving still greater acclaim as the highwayman who actually made the famous ride to York which is traditionally ascribed to Dick Turpin.

The story of these two men, and how the tale of the most famous highway legend of all was credited to the wrong one, will form the next chapter.

8 The Highwayman Who Really Rode to York

Few visitors to the beautiful city of York leave without a detour to the grave of Dick Turpin, today just a worn headstone which lies close to Fishergate, one of the gateways in the city's magnificent circular walls. Countless thousands have stood beside this unprepossessing stone and have probably seen in their mind's eye the dashing and romantic figure of Turpin as he has been portrayed for hundreds of years in words and pictures, in magazines, books, films and on television. Many will perhaps have imagined the young man mounted on his famous horse, Black Bess, her flanks streaked with sweat and her nostrils flaring, as the pair galloped into the city at the end of a remarkable ride from London that is still today the talk of the world.

The truth behind the legend is, however, rather different. For Turpin was not, in fact, the handsome figure of tradition; nor did he own a horse called Black Bess; and he most certainly did not ride at record speed from London to York.

It is a fact, though, that by one of those curious twists of fate which make history so endlessly fascinating – and the history of highwaymen doubly so – that the man who *did* make that famous ride also ended his days in York: but there is no gravestone or even a plaque to commemorate the event. The man's name was John Nevison – 'Swift Nicks' as he became known – a Yorkshireman by birth, a highwayman by calling, and ultimately a felon hanged in the famous city. Though the fiction of Dick Turpin's ride is now a part of the history of highwaymen, the fact belongs to Nevison and for the sake of accuracy their lives must be discussed together. For what Nevison achieved, Turpin was given the credit, and time has continued to acclaim one man at the expense of the other.

History has also shown John Nevison to be something of an enigma, for there is much about his life that is shrouded in mystery. His Christian name, for instance, may have been William rather than John, and there are stories that his surname was not Nevison but perhaps Brace or Johnson. There are those who believe him to have been a rogue and a murderer, while others maintain he deserves the reputation of a latter-day Robin Hood who robbed the rich to pay the poor. And, more puzzling still, did he *really* have a secret meeting with Charles II, who gave him the nickname 'Swift Nicks', as some sources have claimed?

Important evidence of Nevison's fame is, though, to be found in a reference in Macaulay's *History of England* where he is the only highwayman, except Claude Duval, to be mentioned by name – even if his life is summarized in a few terse lines:

> Nevison levied a quarterly tribute on all the northern drovers and, in return, not only spared them himself but protected them against all other thieves; he demanded purses in the most courteous manner; he gave largely to the poor what he had taken from the rich; his life was once spared by royal clemency, but he again tempted fate, and at length died, in 1685, on the gallows of York.

As we shall see, Macaulay has the date of Nevison's death wrong, and is less than specific about the royal meeting, but he certainly cannot be accused of underestimating the highwayman's reputation.

Much confusion has arisen amongst later writers by comparing this report with the colourful and often conflicting accounts of the seventeenth century pamphleteers, so that it is necessary to go back, wherever possible, to original sources to try and establish the real facts. Though various locations have been suggested for his birth, the most probable one is the town of Pontefract, in the year 1640; we do know that he was the only son of a comfortably off wool merchant. At school, Nevison was said to have been a bright student, but given to being 'the ringleader of all his young companions in rudeness and debauchery'.

Other references indicate that he also had a penchant for stealing things such as apples and poultry, but when caught stealing a valuable piece of cutlery he was reported to his schoolmaster and given a terrible thrashing. The rebel in the young boy was apparently roused at this indignity and, taking ten pounds from his father, and a horse that belonged to the schoolmaster, he rode off to London to make a new life. The journey was made on much the same route as that by which he would return rather faster some years later.

Once in the metropolis, Nevison used his best manners to obtain a job as a junior clerk to a brewer, and appears to have held the post quite happily for some three years. At seventeen though, the wanderlust stirred once again, and when he was asked to collect a debt and found himself in possession of over £200, the temptation proved too great. Before nightfall he had taken a passage on a ship bound for Antwerp.

In Holland, Nevison had a brief liaison with a burgher's daughter – who helped him relieve her father of some valuable jewellery and money – but he apparently abandoned her not long afterwards. Next he enlisted in an English regiment under the command of the Duke of York (later James II) serving the Spanish in Flanders, and here he is said to have distinguished himself as a soldier until the force was disbanded. Following this, Nevison decided to return across the Channel and make peace with his family in Pontefract.

Nevison's mother had died in his absence, but it seems he lived quietly with his father until the old gentleman, too, passed on. Having hoped he might come into money, John instead found himself impoverished and, in the words of one of his more reliable biographers, Elizabeth Villiers in *Stand and Deliver: The Romantic Adventures of the High Toby* (1928), he decided to 'take to the road'. Using up the remainder of his assets he bought himself a horse, a sword, a pair of pistols, some boots and spurs and a mask and rode out to start carving his own legend.

Elizabeth Villiers continues:

> As a highwayman he became known as Nick Nevison, though why the name was bestowed upon him is not exactly clear; perhaps he adopted it as an alias, or it may have been bestowed as a left-handed compliment, suggesting he was a relation of 'Old Nick'. He gathered around him a band of kindred spirits, of whom two have come down to fame as his second-in-commands, one a Thomas Tankard of Lincolnshire, and the other a

> good-looking young fellow named Edward Bracey who was a relation of Nevison's.
>
> These three established their headquarters at an old house by the Trent side of Farndon, not far from Newark, where they installed a gipsy woman named Elizabeth Burton to act as their housekeeper, all the while Nevison keeping his home in York, whither he had removed from Pontefract, and being known there as a respectable citizen.
>
> So well organised did the gang become, that they drew regular allowances from the drovers and farmers who used the North Road, the money so paid ensuring the dealers should be free from highway robbery. It is to Nevison's credit that he kept this queer bargain honourably – all who subscribed to his road fund were free to travel without fear, no matter what valuables they might carry. They had paid their toll, therefore the highwayman and his gang did not rob them and took care they were robbed by no others.

In addition to operating this 'queer bargain' – to all intents and purposes a kind of seventeenth century protection racket – Nevison was also a traditional highwayman, and it is said that by the time he was in his middle twenties he had amassed enough money to retire. But, after a short period as a man of leisure, the lure of the road proved too strong and he returned to his old ways.

It was not only his reputation as a successful robber that grew, however; according to another contemporary account, 'in all his pranks he was very favourable to the female sex, who generally gave him the character of a civil, obliging robber'. He was also, says this report, 'charitable to the poor, and, being a true Royalist, he never attempted anything against those of that party'.

But Nevison's career was not without its setbacks. In 1674, he was arrested near Wakefield and thrown into the local gaol – although before charges could be brought he cleverly escaped. Two years later, in March 1676, he was again caught and confined in York Castle on charges of robbery and horse stealing. Once more he outwitted the law by getting himself drafted into a volunteer force bound for Tangier. Just as the party was about to disembark from Tilbury – and the chains had been slipped from his ankles – Nevison jumped overboard and was soon lost in the surrounding countryside.

When Nevison was apprehended a third time in 1681 after a robbery in Leicestershire, the authorities decided to take no chances with such a slippery customer. For by now his reputation as a highwayman had also been butressed by stories of his great escapes, too, and his power of jumping safely from prodigious heights. Some even whispered he had the power to make himself invisible! 'Swift Nicks' must be restrained at all costs, the authorities decided, and the highwayman found himself manacled hand and foot in a closely guarded cell.

But to a man of his ingenuity the situation merely offered another challenge – and he soon hit upon a plan with the help of an associate, who masqueraded as a doctor. Complaining of an illness, Nevison was allowed to see the 'doctor' who announced the poor fellow was dying of the plague. No illness could have struck more fear into the gaolers, and when Nevison was pronounced dead by the same man (who had secretly painted blue spots on the 'corpse' and administered a sleeping draught to emphasize his diagnosis), they could not get the body out of the prison quickly enough. Taken away in a coffin, Nevison, on awaking from the anaesthetic, leapt happily from his temporary confinement and returned once more to the road.

Now his reputation took on a completely new dimension, as Elizabeth Villiers has explained:

> Soon his name was being whispered throughout Yorkshire as that of one whose ghost haunted the ways familiar to him in life. In Leicester Gaol he had died, men said, yet he was seen riding along the high roads. That the figure which thundered by at a gallop was the highwayman's ghost was easy for frightened yokels to believe, but rich farmers, stopped on their way from market and relieved of their wallets, or wealthy travellers who heard the 'Stand and Deliver!' command, were convinced Nevison was in the flesh. The Governor of Leicester Gaol made a shrewd guess at the truth, and was so angry at having been duped, that out of his own pocket he offered a reward of £20 for the capture of the highwayman.

In July 1681 Nevison was very nearly caught again when an innkeeper named Darcy Fletcher attempted to collect the reward on the highwayman's head by slipping a sleeping draught into his beer and then sending word to the authorities. Nevison, however, came to his senses sooner than expected and, realizing what had happened, fought his way out of the trap, killing Fletcher with a pistol shot. It was a narrow escape – but with a death to his name, the net around the highwayman now began to grow tighter.

Elizabeth Burton, the gypsy woman who had been associated with Nevison since the start of his career, appears to have been arrested at about this time, and, turning King's evidence to save her own neck, confessed to the authorities about her role, as well as giving details of the robberies that the highwayman had committed against travellers across an area that included York, Lincoln, Nottingham and Derby.

Although this disclosure can be seen as just one more nail in Nevison's coffin, the final one was also provided by another, unidentified, woman who kept the Plough Inn at Sandal, near Wakefield, where Nevison occasionally stopped after a robbery. In collusion with a certain Captain William Hardcastle who lived nearby, this lady tipped the wink on 6 March 1684 that 'the bird is in the cage', and Nevison was arrested by a party of three armed men and returned once more to York Castle.

On 15 March, following a brief trial in which the evidence was overwhelmingly against him, Nevison was hanged at the appropriately named Knavesmire. He died still protesting his innocence, according to a popular ballad that went on sale immediately afterwards, entitled, *Nevison's Garland*:

> And when then he came to the Bench,
> 'Guilty or Not Guilty' they to him did cry,
> 'Not Guilty,' then Nevison said,
> 'I'm clear e'er since the same day,
> That the King did my Pardon Grant,
> I ne'er did rob anyone, nor kill
> But that Fletcher in all my life,
> 'Twas in my Defence, I say still.'

This mention of a royal pardon is the foundation of the story – repeated by Macaulay – of the meeting between Nevison and Charles II, at which it is said the highwayman was given his nickname: though there is no official record to bear out the claim.

Another publication of the time, *The Yorkshire Robber: or, Captain Hind Improved*, a penny pamphlet, attempted to compare Nevison's achievements with those of the first great highwayman, describing the man from Pontefract as 'a person of quick understanding, tall in stature, every way proportional, exceeding valiant, having also the air and carriage of a gentleman'.

What it curiously makes *no* mention of at all is the highlight of Nevison's career: his ride to York. That, as we shall see, did not find its way into print until 1724 and was thereafter to be appropriated for a quite different legend – the legend of a rather unsavoury young man who was then only a butcher's lad and had not even been born when 'Swift Nicks' performed the feat ...

The myth of Dick Turpin has been told in countless versions, the 'facts' about his life, though, are rather different.

It is perhaps fitting for a man whose name so dominates the history of highwaymen that Richard Turpin should have been born in a tavern, the Bell Inn, in the pretty Essex village of Hempstead. For, as we have seen, these places were frequently used by highway robbers as somewhere to hide and dispose of their spoils. The historian Macaulay has commented on such inns:

> Their criminal connivance, it was affirmed, enabled banditti to infest the roads with impunity. That these suspicions were not without foundation is proved by the dying speeches of some penitent robbers of that age.

Turpin's birthplace, in fact, still exists today, although it is now known as the Rose and Crown, and is believed to be one of the longest established English pubs, liquor having been served there since the sixteenth century. In the parish church of Hempstead, the register confirms that Richard Turpin, the infant son of John and Mary Turpin, was baptized there on 21 September 1705.

John Turpin was the keeper of the Bell and a reasonably prosperous man who encouraged his son to learn to read and write, under the tutelage of the local schoolmaster, John Smith. The older Turpin also paid for the boy to be instructed in the trade of a butcher in Whitechapel, before helping him set up on his own account at the age of twenty-one in nearby Waltham Abbey.

Richard Turpin prospered at his trade and his reputation grew. He took a wife, another publican's daughter named Hester Palmer, and all seemed set fair for a comfortable existence – until it was discovered that he had sold some meat from stolen cattle. Most accounts of Dick's life at this time claim he was rustling cattle and sheep on a scale that an American cowboy would have envied: in fact, the records show that the number of beasts without bills of sale which turned him from a trader to a criminal was just two!

It is not true, either, that this exposure drove him straight on to the road as a highwayman. Certainly, though, he left the district and was next heard of on Canvey Island, Essex, where he apparently saw profit to be made in the flourishing smuggling trade. By all accounts he had grown into a rather coarse-looking man – 'his face very much marked with small pox', to quote one newspaper description – who dressed badly, and was already showing signs of the deceit and cowardice which his biographers would later choose to ignore.

Although Dick became involved in the smuggling trade on the Essex marshes, he took as few personal risks as possible – sometimes choosing to snatch the spoils of other smugglers by presenting himself as a king's revenue man when they returned from trips with their spoils. He was also apparently not above informing on a gang with whom he might well have been involved himself, if the profit from betrayal was likely to be higher than the sale of the contraband itself! Perhaps not surprisingly, Turpin did not persist in this occupation for long, as he came to fear increasingly the vengeance of the smugglers he had cheated.

After a short period as a deer-poacher back in his old haunts around Waltham Abbey – where his skill as a butcher and his ability to 'fence' the carcases to unscrupulous dealers increased his revenue – Turpin decided to set his criminal sights somewhat higher. To this end he got together with a group of like-minded rogues and began a period terrorizing highway travellers and robbing prosperous householders in the home counties. His cowardly streak also became more evident when he deliberately absented himself from some of the more dangerous raids – though he still demanded his share of the proceeds.

A predilection for gratuitous violence and sadism was similarly noticed when he and his men took to seizing servants who refused to give information about the whereabouts of their masters' valuables and threatening to roast them over a fire until they talked. One widow's refusal to reveal where she kept her money provoked Turpin to one of his few authentically recorded utterances: 'God damn your blood, you old bitch, if you won't tell us I'll set your arse on the grate!'

A few days after this, the same crew carried out a robbery of appalling violence and rape which, in the light of the glamour which has come to surround Turpin's life, makes very salutory reading. A report of the event was actually carried in the *London Evening Post* of February 1735 and reads as follows:

> On Tuesday night about 8 o'clock, five villains came to the house of Mr. Lawrence, a farmer of Edgwaresbury, near Edgware in Middlesex, but the door being bolted they could not get in, so they went to the boy who was in the sheep-house and compelled him to call the maid who opened the door; upon which they rushed in, bound the master, maid and one man-servant, and swore they would murder all the family if they did not discover their money, etc; they trod the bedding under foot, in case there should be money hidden in it, and took about £10 in money, linen, etc, all they could lay their hands on; they broke the old man's head, dragged him about the house, emptied a kettle of water from the fire over him, and ravished the maid, Dorothy Street, using her in a most barbarous manner, and then went off leaving the family bound, locked the door and took the key with them.

The following day's issue of the *Post* provided a painful footnote by revealing that the paper had learned that when the five men failed to find as much money as they had expected, 'they let Mr. Lawrence's breeches down and set him bare on the fire several times which burnt him prodigiously'.

The catalogue of Turpin's crimes at this period of his life is full of such incidents, similarly sordid and brutal, all demonstrating the callousness of which he was capable. According to this evidence, 1735 marked the high point of the gang's activities, when they were committing on average one robbery a week and making forays as far as Surrey, Kent, Hertfordshire, and even occasionally back into Turpin's native Essex.

A reward of £100 for each of the gang was soon on offer, and a tip-off resulted in the five men being cornered in a Westminster public house which they frequented. A short fight ensued and somehow, in the mêlée, Turpin managed to escape by jumping out of a window and on to the back of a conveniently waiting horse. He quickly fled the city, leaving his erstwhile partners to their fate – and an unanswerable question as to whether he might just have masterminded the whole arrest himself.

For a while Turpin laid low – being supplied with clothes and food by the ever loyal Hester – and then, in October 1735, he ventured out on the road at Stamford Hill and had a most surprising encounter. Charles Harper has described what happened:

> Observing a well-dressed and well-mounted stranger riding slowly along, Turpin spurred up to him, presented a pistol and demanded his money. The stranger merely laughed, which threw Turpin into a passion, and he threatened him with instant death if he did not comply. The other laughed again and said, 'What dog eat dog? Come brother Turpin, if you don't know me I know you and I shall be glad of your company.

The man was none other than Tom King, a highwayman like Dick himself, and also carrying a price on his head. He and 'the renowned Butcher-Highwayman', as the papers were now referring to Turpin, decided to join forces. They also agreed to find a hideout from which to carry out their highway robberies, and it was almost certainly King who picked a hideout in Epping Forest with an unobscured view along the road to London. This famous spot has since been located between the Loughton road and the Kings Oak public house.

The partnership proved a fruitful one – though not every potential victim was so afraid of Turpin that they did not try to defy him, as a fascinating newspaper clipping from the *Country Journal* of 23 April 1737 reveals:

> On Saturday last as a gentleman of West Ham and others were travelling to Epping the famous Turpin and a new companion of his came up and attacked the coach in order to rob it; the gentleman had a carbine in the coach, loaded with slugs, and seeing them coming, got it ready, and presented it at Turpin, on stopping the coach, but it flashed in the pan; upon which says Turpin, 'God damn you, you have missed me, but I won't miss you,' and shot into the coach at him, passing between him and a lady in the coach; and then they rode off towards Ongar, and dined afterwards at Hare Street, and robbed in the evening several passengers in the Forest between Loughton and Romford who knew him.

In the following month, Turpin added murder to his other crimes when he shot and killed a forest-keeper named Thomas Morris who had tracked him back to the hideout. Realizing now that their hideaway had been spotted, the pair quickly took themselves off to London.

Although there are conflicting reports about the end of the partnership, the most authentic story says they were cornered near an inn on the Whitechapel road. When one of the lawmen grabbed King as he was dismounting, the highwayman immediately turned to Turpin who was still on his horse and shouted, 'Dick, shoot him or we are taken, by God.'

Turpin did indeed fire – but only succeeded in hitting King. Seeing this, he wheeled and rode off into the night with his partner's curses ringing in his ears. The luckless King was later executed at Tyburn.

Perhaps it was the fate of his associate – or more likely the realization that the law's net was closing around him – which made Turpin decide to move north. His years of successful crime had left him with some money and he decided to use this to adopt the role of a gentleman horse-dealer in Yorkshire.

So, in the spring of 1737 he headed north, travelling through Suffolk into Lincolnshire and finally into Yorkshire – a journey not achieved in a day as the legend would have us believe; but cautiously, with an eye always open for any sign of pursuit, and over several months.

Perhaps, as he ambled northwards, 'John Palmer' – as Turpin was now calling himself – saw one of the notices being posted for his arrest, and, well aware of how often he had double-crossed associates in the past, realized he was leaving his old haunts only just in time.

> His Majesty was pleased to promise his most gracious pardon to any of the accomplices of Richard Turpin who shall discover him, so that he may be apprehended and convicted of the Murder, or any of the Robberies he has committed; as likewise a reward of £200 to any person or persons who shall discover the said criminal so that he may be apprehended and convicted as aforesaid, over and above all other rewards to which they may be entitled.

Despite such a clear warning, Turpin was too much of a dyed-in-the-wool villain to change his ways for long. And, though his knowledge of horseflesh and his well-filled purse enabled him to settle at Welton, near Beverley in October 1737, and live the life of a gentleman, a year later, suspicions that 'Mr Palmer' might well be the person behind the spate of horse stealings in the district, became a conviction. Despite Palmer's/Turpin's protests, he was arrested on 16 October 1738 on suspicion of robbery, and conveyed to York Castle to await trial. By pure chance he was put into the very same cell that John Nevison had occupied fifty-five years previously.

However, the highwayman might well have kept his real identity a secret if he had not decided the following February to write to his brother-in-law in Hempstead asking for help to secure his release. When the letter was seen, quite by chance, by Turpin's former schoolmaster, James Smith, who still lived in the village, he immediately recognized the handwriting. Well aware that there was a £200 reward on offer for his former pupil, Smith hurried off to the authorities with his information.

When the news reached the general population of York of just *who* was locked up in their castle, thousands flocked to see the famous Turpin. And, probably realizing the game was now up, Dick himself began to behave for the first time as legend would have us believe he had behaved all his life.

During the trial of 'John Palmer alias Paumer, alias Richard Turpin' – to quote the indictment – which began at the York assizes on 22 March 1739, Dick conducted himself with considerable composure, and similarly showed great dignity when the inevitable verdict of death was pronounced. He spent the last twenty-six days after his sentencing 'in joking, drinking with the many visitors who came to see him, and telling stories of his adventures', to quote a contemporary broadsheet. Interestingly, one of these visitors is said to have sworn that the prisoner was not Turpin at all – which prompted the last of the highwayman's recorded utterances: 'Lay him the wager,' he told his gaoler, 'and I'll go you halves!'

The *York Courant* of 10 April 1739 has provided an eye-witness account of how Turpin met his death on the morning of 7 April, aged thirty-four; when, once more out of character, he took a leaf from the lives of some of his great predecessors in highway history, and decided to die with dignity. The terror of the southern counties bought himself a brand new suit of clothes and hired five men to wear black hatbands and ride through York with him to the Knavesmire. On the way he 'bowed and flourished his hat to the ladies like a hero'.

Arriving at the place of execution, the *Courant* goes on,

> he behaved with the greatest assurance to the last. It was very remarkable that as he mounted the ladder his right leg trembled, on which he stamped it down with an air, and with undaunted courage looked round about him, and after speaking a few words to the topsman, he threw himself off the ladder and expired in about five minutes. Before his death, he declared himself to be the notorious highwayman Turpin and confessed to the topsman a great number of robberies which he had committed.

Perhaps, it could be argued with hindsight, Turpin's brave end did much to turn what had been a villainous life into the stuff of melodrama for later generations. In fact, the explanation is far simpler than that, and the transformation of his character, and the addition to his legend of the ride to York, is attributable to the pens of just two men: Daniel Defoe and W. Harrison Ainsworth.

An examination of all the contemporary records of Dick Turpin's life and career reveals not a line about any mad dash over the 190 miles from London to York. In fact, the ride was already on record in 1724 when young Dick was only an apprentice butcher in Whitechapel – it is to be found in *A Tour Through The Whole Island of Great Britain* by Daniel Defoe (1661–1731), famous for *Robinson Crusoe* (1719) and less well known as the son of a butcher!

Defoe, a social historian as well as a novelist, first heard about the ride of John 'Swift Nicks' Nevison from local stories while on his journey, and then investigated the amazing story further so as to recount it to his readers. This account is worth repeating in full to establish once and for all Nevison's claim to have made the ride to York.

> From Gravesend we see nothing remarkable on the road from Gad's Hill, a noted place for robbing seamen after they have received their pay at Chatham. Here it was a famous robbery was committed in the year 1676. It was about four o'clock in the morning when a gentleman was robbed by one 'Nicks', on a bay mare, just on the declining part of the hill, on the west side, for he swore to the spot and to the man. Mr. Nicks, who robbed him, came away to Gravesend, was stopped by the difficulty of the

boat, and of the passage, near an hour, which was a great discouragement to him, but was a kind of bait to his horse. From thence he rode across the county of Essex, through Tilbury, Horndon, and Billericay to Chelmsford; here he stopped about half an hour to refresh his horse, and give him some balls; from thence to Braintree, Bocking, Wethersfield; then over the downs to Cambridge, and from thence, keeping still to the cross roads, he went by Fenny Stanton to Godmanchester and Huntingdon, where he baited himself and his mare about an hour.

Then, holding on the north road, and keeping a full larger gallop most of the way, he came to York that same afternoon, put off his boots and riding clothes, and went dressed as if he had been an inhabitant of the place, not a traveller, to the bowling green, where, among other gentlemen, was the Lord Mayor of the city; he, singling out his Lordship, studied to do something particular that the Mayor might remember him by, and accordingly lays some odd bet with him concerning the bowls then running, which should cause the Mayor to remember it the more particularly, and takes occasion to ask his Lordship what o'clock it was; who, pulling out his watch, told him the hour, which was a quarter before or a quarter after eight at night. Some other circumstances, it seems, he carefully brought into their discourse which should make the Lord Mayor remember the day of the month exactly, as well as the hour of the day.

Upon a prosecution which happened afterwards for this robbery, the whole merit of the case turned upon this single point. The person robbed swore as above to the man, to the place, and to the time, in which the fact was committed – namely, that he was robbed on Gad's Hill in Kent, on such a day, and at such a time of the day, and on such a part of the hill, and that the prisoner at the bar was the man that robbed him. Nicks, the prisoner, denied the facts, called several persons to his reputation, alleged that he was as far off as Yorkshire at that time, and that particularly, the day whereon the prosecution swore he was robbed, he was at bowls on the public green in the city of York; and to support this he produced the Lord Mayor of York to testify that he was so, and that the Mayor acted so and so with him there as above. This was so positive and so well attested that the jury acquitted him on a bare supposition that it was impossible the man could be at two places so remote on one and the same day.

Defoe also adds an interesting postscript:

There are more particulars related of this story, such as I do not take upon me to affirm – namely, that King Charles II prevailed

> on him, an assurance of pardon and that he should not be brought into any further trouble about it, to confess the truth to him privately, and that he owned to His Majesty that he committed the robbery, and how he rode the journey after it, and that upon this the King gave him the name or title of 'Swift Nicks'.

While this account certainly adds a little evidence to the debate concerning the royal connection with Nevison's nickname, it undeniably confirms the ride to York: a ride of roughly 220 miles in fifteen hours. And there the story might have ended had another writer not decided to combine it with a fictionalized version of Dick Turpin's life.

William Harrison Ainsworth (1805–1882) was a Victorian solicitor turned author who specialized in 'fictionalising' the lives of notorious historical figures such as prison escaper Jack Sheppard and the conspirator Guy Fawkes, who gave their names to works of 1839 and 1831, and the seventeenth century women brought to trial for witchcraft, described in *The Lancashire Witches* (1848). But it is to his highly coloured version of Dick Turpin's life (rather curiously entitled *Rookwood* (1834)), that the ghost of the highwayman owes his glorious reputation.

Ainsworth deleted Turpin's villainous character from previous accounts and instead produced a romantic figure in gold-braid coat and cocked hat who, pursued by the chief constable of Westminster and other agents of the law, rides on a magnificent horse called Black Bess from Hornsey to York. In a melodramatic finale, Turpin reaches York just as the bell of the Minster clock is striking six and his horse drops dead of exhaustion beneath him. Animal lovers everywhere could hardly fail to be moved at the scene of the heartbroken Turpin weeping over the body of the gallant animal that had carried him to freedom.

The author later claimed that he wrote the entire episode of the ride to York, close on twenty thousand words, in a single sitting of one day and night, and certainly it 'rattles on in superb style', to use his own words. The public loved Ainsworth's blood-and-thunder tale of the highwayman and many, believing it to be true, saw Turpin – if indeed they had ever *thought* of him before – in a new and heroic light. Ainsworth shrugged off the complaints of a number of contemporary historians that he had distorted the truth, insisting he had drawn a composite figure utilizing various sources (including, as we have seen, Defoe's account of John Nevison); at no time did he claim the book was true. Turpin's horse, Black Bess, he added, was pure invention in name and breeding – though within years of his death, it has to be said, a public house, the Black Horse Inn on Westminster Broadway was being claimed as the place from which the ride started, while the sign commemorated the animal that had once been stabled there!

The fact remains that *Rookwood* turned one of the eighteenth century's worst criminals into an immortal: a courageous, daring and kindly outlaw of the road; a man of the people defying oppressive laws. And so he has remained, each passing generation adding a little more gloss to the story, as other novelists have piled improbability upon impossibility to place Turpin forever among the ranks of England's greatest heroes.

Such revelations as are given here, though, will do nothing to damage the legend of Dick Turpin, so firmly is it now entrenched in the public mind. But, surely, John Nevison deserves more than the footnote he is usually afforded in the history of highwaymen – if for nothing more than what was one of the most brilliant feats of horsemanship and endurance on record.

9 The Wicked Ladies

Before leaving the seventeenth century, a chapter must be devoted to the female highway robbers who plundered the roads of England. It would be quite wrong, in fact, to imagine that the holding up of travellers at this time was a wholly male preserve, or that the only place women have in this history is as the mistresses (or 'doxies') of the men of the road. There were, indeed, quite a number of women, of both high and low rank, attracted by the glamour and danger of the life.

The 'doxy', it is true, had an important role to play in the highwayman's life. For apart from being sexual companions, these women were expected to keep an eye open for danger in the shape of pursuers, while those who worked in taverns and inns could listen out for potential victims. It has been said with more than a little truth that, to a highwayman, a faithful mistress was second only in importance to a good horse! There were also, though, other ladies who wanted more from life than just to stay put and hear all about the excitement of highway robbery at second hand …

A number of readers may already have heard of Lady Catherine Ferrers, the beautiful seventeenth-century lady of the manor who rode out under the cover of darkness from her home at Markyate near Hemel Hempstead to rob travellers on their way to and from London. Her exploits have been recounted in a number of books and two very successful films both entitled *The Wicked Lady*: the first made in 1945 starring the British actress, Margaret Lockwood, and the second in 1983 featuring the American, Faye Dunaway. But Lady Ferrers was only one of several such women of the road whose part in the history of the highwayman has tended to be overlooked or minimized: for these women, the progeny of the legendary Moll Cutpurse, were often every bit as clever, daring and successful as their male counterparts in an occupation that, never let it be forgotten, also demanded such physical attributes as brute strength, and good shooting and riding skills.

It should not be underestimated just how difficult it was to be a highwaywoman in the seventeenth century, for, as Elizabeth Villers has pointed out, they were immediately handicapped by their clothes and the manner in which they had to ride a horse:

> The dress worn by women during the century and a half through which the true highwaymen flourished did not lend itself to athletic exercise. When women rode it was on pillions, chairs strapped to the cruppers of heavy draught horses, or if they were daring enough to use the side saddle and to manage their horses alone, they were looked upon as wonders of bravery – *vide* Scott's Diana Vernon. Further, they were restricted by the extraordinary length and weight of the habits they were doomed to wear, as well as by the fact that their saddles had only pommels set opposite each other. In such a saddle a woman had no grip, so was easily unseated by the stumble of her mount, while for any girl to hint at riding astride would have been considered the height of impropriety.

Although Elizabeth Villiers argues that these are the main reasons why 'highway robbery was not popular with the fair sex', she does not deny that there *were* some females who overcame the odds – referring to a handful including Joan Phillips and Margaret Matthews (whom we shall study later). She makes another interesting comment about female criminals during this period:

> The *Newgate Calendar* and similar records contain long lists of female criminals. Approximately as many women as men died at Tyburn and other places of public execution, and in Johnson's *Lives of the Highwaymen* are included, 'The German Princess' and 'Nan of Hertford', but they were not highwaywomen, they were adventuresses to whose class belong the Yorkshire Witch and Jenny Diver and many another law-breaking female. It was in the streets and the byeways of the cities that these carried on their nefarious trades as pickpockets and sneak-thieves. Not for them were the dashing adventures of the King's Highway.

While I am in agreement with much that Elizabeth Villiers says, I do believe she is misrepresenting the facts to make the point that 'The German Princess' and 'Nan of Hertford' (she actually means Nan Hereford) were not highway robbers. There is evidence that proves they both *were*. (Again, we shall be considering them later in this chapter.)

Patrick Pringle also shares the view that, regardless of their physical disadvantages, there were some good highwaywomen on the English roads:

> Sometimes they worked as partners with men, but they were no more doxies than a lady doctor is a nurse. They carried pistols and wore masks and bade travellers stand and deliver in the traditional way. They also wore men's clothes and took great care to conceal their sex – for obvious reasons. The highwayman's success depended more on his ability to scare his victims than to shoot straight. So highwaywomen, like the lady novelists, had to practise their profession under a masculine *nom de guerre* if they wanted to be taken seriously.

It seems highly probable that even before the end of Moll Cutpurse's long and successful career – which ended, as one writer put it, 'at the bad old age of seventy-five in 1659' – there were other women who resorted to highway robbery. But the first of the 'wicked ladies' of whom we have detailed evidence is Joan Phillips, born in 1656, and brought to as bad an end as Moll Cutpurse, in 1685.

Joan was the daughter of a wealthy Northamptonshire farmer named John Phillips who lavished money and affection on her as she grew into a beautiful, blonde-haired young woman. Among her many admirers was an articled clerk working for Mr Phillips, named Edward Bracey, who also came from a good local family. However, when the boy found his love returned and approached his master for Joan's hand in marriage he was rudely – and perhaps unfairly, considering his background – turned down.

The girl was heartbroken at her father's refusal, but Edward said he had a plan: they would run away together and start a new life. Joan, always a practical girl, pointed out that any apprentice who broke his indenture, as Edward was proposing to do, risked very serious punishment. The besotted Edward replied that any risk was worth taking for her, and in any event he planned to take her to Yorkshire where he had a cousin, a man of wealth and importance, whom he was sure would help. His name was John Nevison – the very same 'Swift Nicks'.

The couple rode north to Yorkshire, Joan disguised in a suit of Edward's old clothing, and they were indeed received kindly by Nevison. The destitute couple were not long in learning their new benefactor's occupation and needed little encouragement to follow in his footsteps. Joan decided to continue wearing her lover's clothing as well as adopting the name of 'John', thereby preserving the nature of her sex from Nevison's accomplices as well as their victims.

According to a contemporary report: 'These two sparks who lived by the scaring words, "Stand and deliver", frequently robbed together, Bracey's wife appearing in man's apparel whenever they robben coaches in Yorkshire and Nottinghamshire.' (Although Joan was described as Mrs Bracey when leading her 'alternative' life, there is no indication that the couple ever married.)

Captain Alexander Smith has written of this highwaywoman:

> She was often hampered for her notorious thefts, and was once or twice in great danger of hanging. She and her husband having got a great deal of money by their ruining honest people, they set up an inn in the suburbs of Bristol. And Joan being a very handsome woman, her beauty brought her a great many guests, who spent a great deal of money to obtain her favour. But all to no purpose, for though she seemed to give them encouragement, yet being constant to her first spark, she gulled them all in the end, and exposed them to open shame.

One particularly ardent admirer, a Mr Dacey, lost both his money and his clothes by trying to inveigle the strong-willed Joan into bed. This came about when, tiring of the man's constant, suggestive remarks, she finally agreed to sleep with him one night when, she said, her husband would be away. Mr Dacey was to come to her room at midnight wearing only his nightshirt and she would 'satisfy his every pleasure'. Following these instructions carefully, Dacey entered Joan's room only to find Edward there brandishing a sword – with which the highwayman drove the unfortunate man from the inn, minus everything but the shirt he stood up in!

Records give no indication as to how many robberies Joan Phillips carried out on her own or with Bracey – but it was a lone enterprise that was to be her undoing in the spring of 1685. The event occurred on the Loughborough road near Nottingham when she brought to a halt an expensive-looking coach and four, inside which sat 'a person of quality' who also proved to be a brave man.

Demanding that he hand over his valuables, Joan was just on the point of checking her spoils when the man sprang out of the carriage and dealt her such a hard blow that she fell from her horse. Winded as their assailant was by the fall, the gentleman and his coach-driver had no trouble in restraining her. It was not, however, until Joan had been taken to the prison in Nottingham that her sex was discovered.

The revelation that 'John Phillips', the highwayman who had stalked the Midlands countryside, was actually a woman was greeted with amazement by the press and public alike, and the local assizes was packed with spectators when Joan stood her trial. Her beauty undoubtedly softened many male hearts in the courtroom – but not the judge's. She was sentenced to hang on 15 April.

According to a local tradition which is still repeated in Nottingham, Joan Phillips was executed at the end of Wilford Lane; afterwards her body was taken away by some friends to be buried in a small village in Sherwood Forest. Edward Bracey watched the hanging of his beloved in the most abject despair. Captain Alexander Smith tells us that he did not long outlive his lover:

> Riding to see his wife interred, he was told by an old woman there that he should not survive her above six days. This prediction fell out true, for being at a little alehouse to refresh himself, the white mare he used to rob on was standing at the door, and being known by some passengers, the country was up and surprised him, and before he could mount they discharged at him, the first shot taking off all his fingers from both hands, and killing his mare. She being fallen, and he striving to get over the back pales, another discharge was made at him from a fowling piece, into the guts, where he received several great goose-shots, of which wounds in three days' time he ended his wicked life.

It has to be said that if ever there was a story to suggest there could be true love among the highway fraternity then that of Phillips and Bracey surely is it.

There was nothing very romantic, however, about Ann Meders, 'The German Princess' mentioned by Elizabeth

Villiers, who did her utmost to cheat and defraud every man who crossed her path – and was described by one contemporary report as 'not to be paralleled by the past or present for wickedness'. She was a kind of confidence trickster who preyed on unsuspecting men and turned to highway robbery only when her need for money became desperate.

Ann, who was born on 11 January 1643, was actually the daughter of a chorister in Canterbury Cathedral, but later claimed to have been born at Cologne in Germany, the daughter of Henry Van Wolway, the Lord of Holmstein, from which 'origin' she derived her title. She was apparently a very pretty but solitary child, often burying herself in books of romances and dreaming of being a princess. As a woman, however, she became cold-hearted and grasping: her character doubtless influenced by being unable to attract the kind of high-born man who could fulfil her ambitions for status.

Although the details of her early life are far from clear, it appears she married three times in quick succession – first a shoemaker in Canterbury, then a surgeon in Dover and lastly a man-about-town in London named John Carleton – without ever having divorced either the first or the second husbands! When these facts did become known, Ann fled from England and made her way to 'the much-longed-after city of Cologne', according to a contemporary source. There she began to cheat and steal from gullible citizens and shopkeepers who believed her to be a society lady from England.

In 1663, 'The German Princess', as she now called herself, returned to London, where she once more set herself up in style by duping a number of admirers – both young men and old – with promises of her body in return for their fortunes. Once she had exhausted these men's pockets she would have nothing more to do with them, frequently changing her address to avoid both former lovers and current creditors.

It was Ann's insatiable need for money to live in the best circles that turned her to highway robbery. One night an aged suitor left her apartment in Cheapside after having foolishly revealed to her that he was carrying over £200 in gold coins in his coach. The lady called for her own carriage and, telling her coachman what was in her mind, sped after the old roué.

Although there are no precise details of the hold-up that followed, it is believed that 'The German Princess' levelled a pistol at her victim, demanded his money, and then threatened to tell his wife of his indiscretion with her if he breathed a word of what had happened.

The success of this venture encouraged Ann to use the technique again with other married men who fell for her charms, and she is believed to have committed at least three similar robberies in Covent Garden, Smithfield and Westminster, aided on each occasion by the faithful coach-driver who, one assumes, shared in the spoils and kept silent.

While it is certainly true that Ann Meders did not disguise herself as a man and ride on horseback to hold up her victims, her crimes were certainly highway robberies; they could well be said to have initiated a new variation on the highwayman's traditional method.

Ann's downfall was brought about when she was arrested for the much more mundane crime of stealing a piece of silver-plate from a house in Chancery Lane. As a result, she found herself in the dock at the Old Bailey just before Christmas in 1672, and, according to one report, made the event rather like a theatrical performance by appearing in the most splendid low-cut red and gold dress which covered very little of her ample breasts.

Despite a most beguiling performance, however, she was found guilty. But she had one more card to play, and tried to avoid her fate by using one of the oldest of all female criminals' tricks, 'pleading her belly' (claiming that she was pregnant). However, a jury of women were brought in to confirm this statement and found it untrue. Ann was dispatched to Tyburn on the morning of 2 January 1673, aged thirty.

Pamphlets which appeared after her death described the chorister's daughter as a 'cheat, a jilt and a thief', and if she had not deserved her title in life, it was certainly preserved for her afterwards when – like Moll Cutpurse – her life was featured in a play entitled *The German Princess* by John Holden, which delighted many London theatregoers, including Samuel Pepys who mentioned it in his famous diary.

Nan Hereford, whom Elizabeth Villiers mistakenly calls 'Nan of Hertford', had none of Ann Meders' pretentions to nobility, but was an equally premeditated criminal who 'got money from people by several cunning stratagems', according to a newspaper report of 1690. One of these stratagems was highway robbery.

She was born in 1662 of 'very honest parents' at Ipswich,

Suffolk, but as both had died by the time she was seventeen, Nan travelled to London and found herself a job in service. By all accounts she quickly fell into bad company and, losing her job through stealing, joined a gang of young thieves of both sexes who lived in Westminster and were organized by a Fagin-like old woman called Mrs Wells.

Nan was initially sent to steal from shops and gentlemen's pockets, but was later put into partnership with a boy called Kirkham to hold up inebriated swells returning home from their clubs late at night. Growing tired of the meagre returns to be had from this form of robbery, the boy suggested he and Nan should go on the highway and hold up coaches. 'But,' says a newspaper report:

> in his first attempt in that way of living, he was apprehended and sent to Newgate, afterwards hanged at Tyburn. However, Nan escaped and followed this trade, and in six years did as much damage to the travellers in and about London as £4,000 would not make good.

These few details suggest an amazingly successful career for Nan Hereford, but there is regrettably no more information on any specific robberies or even the manner and dress in which she carried them out. There are merely a few more intriguing lines on how her career ended – suggesting she had a gang of accomplices, tried bribing a witness and even attempted fire-raising to escape punishment – which again makes one yearn for more facts.

> But, at last, going in a sedan with half a dozen sham footmen to attend her, as if she had been a person of quality, she was detected in trying to rob the coach of a linen draper from Cornhill and committed to Newgate. And knowing she had a most rigorous adversary to deal with (because he would not compound the felony although she proferred him a hundred guineas to throw in a bill of *Ignoramus* against it) and that she would certainly be cast for her life, she endeavoured to make her escape by setting Newgate on fire. But being discovered and put out, she was loaded with heavy irons and handcuffed till she came to her trial, when being condemned for firing the aforesaid gaol she was hanged before it, in Newgate Street, on December 22, 1690, aged 28 years, and her body given to the surgeons to be anatomised.

For my money Nan Hereford was not only a highwaywoman but a memorable one at that!

There are rather more details of another Suffolk girl who took to the road and inadvertently confronted one of East Anglia's most notorious highwaymen in 1685. The girl's name was Margaret Matthews and the man she attempted to rob was Thomas Rumbold, a former bricklayer's apprentice from Ipswich, who had held up the Earl of Oxford at Maidenhead Thicket and taken £200 in gold coins from him. Rumbold was also said to have stolen £1,400 from the Archbishop of Canterbury by pretending he had to play dice with the Devil – though this story is widely believed to be apocryphal.

Margaret Matthews was probably born in Lavenham in about 1660, the daughter of a sword-maker. Her story is related by another of the biographers of highwaymen, Captain Charles Johnson, in his account of the exploits of Thomas Rumbold in his *General History of the Most Famous Highwaymen* (1734).

According to Johnson, Rumbold was riding along a lonely road in the direction of London and had just passed a thick coppice when a figure appeared from the trees and commanded him to 'Stand and Deliver!'. Although momentarily startled at finding himself as victim rather than victimizer, Rumbold gave the impression of fumbling in his pockets for some money, but instead drew his pistol and fired at his adversary. The shot was immediately returned, but both bullets missed their targets, instead striking the respective riders' horses and pitching the pair of them on to the ground. Both then drew their swords, and, Captain Johnson reports:

> After hard fighting on both sides, Rumbold finally threw his adversary, bound him hand and foot and proceeded to his more immediate object of rifling. Upon opening his coat he was amazed to discover that he had been fighting with a woman!

Whatever else he may have been, Rumbold on this occasion played the gentleman and, freeing his prisoner, delivered an 'eloquent speech' which his biographer quotes verbatim:

> 'Pardon me, most courageous Amazon, for thus rudely dealing with you; it was nothing but ignorance that caused this error; for could my dim-sighted soul have distinguished what you were, the great love and respect I bear your sex would have deterred

> me from contending with you. But I esteem this ignorance of mine as the greatest happiness since knowledge, in this case, might have deprived me of the opportunity of knowing there could be so much valour in a woman. For your sake, I shall for ever retain a very high esteem for the worst of females.'

Thanking Rumbold for releasing her, Margaret Matthews told him who she was and invited him to return to her home. This proved to be a very isolated house where, over a meal, Margaret explained how she had come to be a highway robber.

Her father's profession had given her a love of swordplay, she said, and she had much preferred lessons at fencing than any domestic chores. At fifteen she had married an innkeeper and been very happy for two years, until the man's violent temper had begun to make her life a misery. With thoughts of escaping from this drudgery, but having no money of her own, 'I adopted the resolution of borrowing a purse occasionally', she explained.

Captain Johnson quotes the highwaywoman further:

> 'I judged this resolution safe enough, if I were not detected in the very act; for who could suspect me to be a robber, wearing abroad man's apparel, but at home a dress more suitable to my sex? Besides, no one could procure better information, or had more frequent opportunities than myself, for, keeping an inn, who could ascertain what booty their guest carried with them better than their landlady?
>
> 'As you can vouch, sir, I knew myself not to be destitute of courage; what, then, could hinder me from entering on such enterprises? Having thus resolved, I soon provided myself with the necessary habiliments for my scheme, carried it into immediate execution, and continued with great success, never having failed until now. Instead of riding to market, or travelling five or six miles about some piece of business (the usual pretence with which I blinded my husband) I would, when out of sight, take the road to the house in which we are now, where I metamorphosed myself and proceeded back again in search of prey.'

Though Captain Johnson gives no specific details about any of Margaret's robberies or how much she made, the fact she was eventually able to maintain an establishment of her own indicates her proceeds must have been substantial. He also has much delight in telling how Margaret got her own back on her husband by ambushing him and robbing him of a large sum of money, which he apparently handed over in such an abject manner that she realized his temper had been merely a disguise for terrible cowardice.

Before the lady could go on with her life story, however, an interruption took place which proved even more intriguing – though the finale was to reveal Thomas Rumbold to be less of a gentleman than he pretended. A servant entered the room where the couple were dining and informed Margaret that two gentlemen were outside.

> At this, our heroine left the room, and returning with her friends, apologised to our adventurer for the interruption, but hoped he would not find the company of her acquaintance disagreeable, whom he soon discovered to be likewise females in disguise!
>
> The conversation became general, and, upon condition of Rumbold stopping all night with them, the Amazon promised to finish her narrative next day. This accorded with the wishes of Rumbold; and when they retired to rest, he found the same room was destined for them all. His curiosity was, however, overcome by his covetousness; for, rising early next morning, and finding all his companions asleep, he rifled their pockets of a considerable quantity of gold and decamped with great expedition, thus disappointing the reader in the continuation of a narrative almost incredible from its singularity.

Sadly, one searches in vain for any further evidence about Margaret Matthews and her circle of highwaywomen, and some writers have cast doubt upon the whole episode, even on the existence of Margaret herself. However, there is evidence of the lady and her career in a number of Suffolk documents, which also record her death from dropsy in Norwich in 1688. Not for her the detection, arrest and execution for crime that Thomas Rumbold suffered at Tyburn a year later in 1689.

Anne Holland, our next subject, was a very different woman indeed from Margaret Matthews: 'though but young, yet could she wheedle most cunningly, lie confoundedly, drink and smoke everlastingly, whore insatiately and brazen out all her actions impudently', according to a broadsheet published at the time of her execution. Her claim for inclusion in these pages is that she also rode out as a highway robber with her husband, James Wilson.

Wilson is similarly portrayed in the broadsheet publication as a rather remarkable figure:

> He was an eminent highwayman, very expert in his occupation, for he was never without false beards, vizards, patches, wens or mufflers, to disguise the natural physiognomy of his face. He knew how to give the watch-word for his comrades to fall on their prey; how to direct them to make their boots dirty, as if they had ridden many miles, when they are not far from their private place of rendezvous: and how to cut the girths and bridles of them whom they rob, and bind them fast in a wood, or some other obscure place. But these pernicious actions justly bringing him to be hanged in a little time, at Maidstone in Kent, Anne was left a hempen widow and forced to shift for herself again.

There are few details of the early life of Anne Holland beyond the fact she was a rather pretty, genteel-looking girl born in London, and such was the variety of pseudonyms she used that her surname could equally well have been Andrews, Charlton, Edwards, Goddard or Jackson! She appears to have gone into service while still a teenager, but rapidly turned to stealing and whoring. However, on the verge of destitution she managed to get a job serving in a London coffee-house, and there beguiled one of the customers, a comb-maker named French, into marriage. When, however, she gave birth to a child less than six months after their marriage, the enraged Mr French threw her out of his home and his life.

It was shortly after this that Anne met James Wilson and, under his guidance, became his partner in crime. The pair robbed travellers on the outskirts of London as well as in parts of Surrey and Kent, and are said on a number of occasions to have uitilized Wilson's collections of wigs to appear as two men.

By all accounts, Anne's career fell into decline after Wilson's execution, and retribution caught up with her, too, in 1705, when she was arrested for stealing a gold watch and twenty guineas from a Dr Trotter in Moorfields. She was executed in the autumn of that same year.

Another wicked lady, Sarah Davis, was also hanged in 1705, having outlived not one but two highwaymen partners. Born in 1685 in Cripplegate, Sarah also adopted several pseudonyms to cover her criminal tracks, including Harris, Thorn and Gothorn. Although her parents were said to have been 'honest but poor', Sarah was barely in her teens when she was seduced by a highway robber named James Wadsworth who introduced her to his occupation by using her as a decoy to stop carriages in the London suburbs. So proficient did she become, that she graduated to riding as a 'male' with Wadsworth who was known in the criminal fraternity by the nickname 'Jemmy The Mouth'.

Perhaps Wadsworth's soubriquet was well deserved, for in 1702, barely twenty-four years old, he was arrested after committing a felony and burglary in London, and made the one-way trip to Tyburn on 25 September. Finding herself destitute and alone, Sarah visited a number of the inns frequented by highwaymen and had soon found herself a new partner in William Pulman, who was known as 'Norwich Will' after his birthplace.

'Norwich Will' was apparently not much of a partner, for the couple worked the highways for less than six months before he was arrested after robbing a Mr Joseph Edwards of a leather bag containing twenty-five guineas. Sarah, it seems, just slipped away into the maw of London and left her associate to his date at Tyburn on 9 March, 1704. He was twenty-six.

It may have been the hanging of these two men that made Sarah aware of the dangers a highwaywoman faced in the early years of the eighteenth century, for there is no evidence she committed any further hold-ups, turning instead to shoplifting in the Clerkenwell area. She was arrested after stealing from a linen shop, and, though delaying her execution for some months by 'pleading her belly', was hung at Tyburn on the ill-omened day of Friday, 13 July, 1705. She was just twenty years old.

Only three more ladies of the road have been traced in this period: two of very little significance; and the third the now far-famed Lady Catherine Ferrers.

The first of the trio was Mary Blacket who appears to have become a highwaywoman while her sailor husband was at sea – though whether she was hard up or just craved a little excitement, it is difficult to decide. She was the daughter of 'very mean parents', to quote the court records, but was nonetheless educated to read and write, and then went into domestic service. She was apparently well thought of when she left to marry a sailor, but this did not prevent her committing the offence which earns her a place in our history after her man had gone to sea.

There is no indication of whether Mary's hold-up of one

William Whittle 'whom she assaulted on the highway and took a watch value £4 and sixpence in money', on 6 August 1726 was her first robbery; but she certainly did not get far from the scene of her crime in Highgate before being caught. With hindsight, it seems tragic that this comparatively minor crime should have cost her her life at Tyburn the following month.

The story of the second lady robber is even more curious, though the details are scant in the extreme and we have neither a name or a precise location. All there is, in fact, is a paragraph which has been extracted from the pages of the Christmas 1735 issue of the *Gentleman's Magazine*.

> On the 24th of November 1735 a butcher in Essex was rode up to by a woman well mounted on a side saddle, who, to his astonishment, presented a pistol and demanded his money. In amazement he demanded what she meant, and received his answer from a good-looking man who, coming to him on horseback, said he was a brute to deny the lady's request, and enforced his conviction by telling him if he did not gratify her desire immediately he would shoot him through the head. The butcher could not resist an invitation to be gallant when supported by such arguments, and he placed his watch and six guineas in her hand.

There can surely be few more curious instances of a highway robbery team than this pair and it seems possible that the whole episode was a practical joke – though whether the ill-used butcher thought so there is no way of knowing!

Lady Catherine Ferrers was undoubtedly the most remarkable as well as the most beautiful of all the highwaywomen. Flame-haired, with bewitching green eyes and pale cream-coloured skin, she nursed a passion for excitement and adventure which was to culminate in murder and a tragic death.

Catherine was born in 1662, the daughter of a wealthy Hertfordshire landowner, John Worth, whose property in Markyate, near Hemel Hempstead, bordered those of the influential lord of the manor, Sir Ralph Ferrers of Markyate Cell. From his daughter's childhood, Mr Worth nursed the idea of marrying her to Lord Ferrers, in order that she might enjoy the status of a lady with a country mansion and a London town house in Lincoln's Inns Fields. Being a dutiful daughter,

Catherine acceded to her father's wishes but it was not a happy 16-year-old bride who went to the altar. She felt all her natural exuberance, which had been developing as she grew to maturity, was now about to be stifled. And how right she was.

Life at Markyate Cell – once an ancient priory – proved just as boring as Catherine had feared. Her husband was a poor lover, more interested in his lands than his young wife, and no children arrived to occupy Lady Ferrers. For almost five frustating years she endured the dull monotony of this life until a casual remark about a highwayman haunting the local roads put the spark of an idea into her mind. Why shouldn't she ride out under the cover of darkness for a little excitement?

Catherine chose her disguise with care, selecting a long-skirted coat and breeches of dark cloth from a chest of spare men's clothing kept by the house steward. To this she added a large, flat-brimmed beaver hat and mask, some heavy gauntlet gloves and a pair of high, spurred boots. Mounted on her own bay horse and armed with a pistol that her brother had taught her to use years before, she sallied forth on to the roads that she had been familiar with since her childhood.

The wicked Lady Ferrers picked as her first victim her own older sister-in-law, a woman with a viper-like tongue who had delighted in making her life miserable. Indeed, she got the greatest satisfaction in holding up the woman's coach and relieving her of all her jewellery, while the terrified woman pleaded for her life. Catherine was still smiling behind her mask as she crept back into Markyate Cell as stealthily as she had left it.

Feeling more alive than she had done for years, it was all the new highwaywoman could do to restrain her laughter the following morning when she heard tell of the outrage which had been committed on her sister-in-law. For her part, Catherine could hardly wait to repeat the adventure.

Next she decided to venture on to Watling Street, the important road which ran from London through St Albans, Dunstable and Stony Stratford to the north. This time, though, she had no victim in mind and had to wait several hours for a passing coach. Her booty this time consisted of coins to the value of several hundred pounds which she took from a foppish man and his wife who offered not the least resistance to the 'manly' figure who materialized out of the darkness with a cry of 'Stand and deliver!'

There was no holding Catherine now. By day she continued to be the dutiful Lady Ferrers, but by night she was the new terror of the Hertfordshire highways. For these forays she left and returned to Markyate Cell by way of a secret passage from her bedroom to the grounds.

In 1683, however, her career took a dramatic turn when she attempted to rob another solitary traveller and instead found herself looking down the barrel of a pistol.

'Now you son of a bitch,' the other challenged. 'Take that mask off and let's see who has been trespassing on Jerry Jackson's preserves!'

Catherine had unwittingly come face to face with another highwayman and had no alternative but to unmask. It was difficult to tell who was the more surprised as the pair looked at each other in the moonlight.

'Be poxed to it!' the startled Jackson is said to have roared. 'So now our wild ladies are turning bridle-cull.'

Although her heart was beating wildly, Catherine had enough control over her emotions to reply, with a touch of amusement in her voice, 'Sir, I am surprised at your behaviour. Since when has dog taken to eating dog?'

The man's laughter split the night air as he, too, saw the funny side of what had happened. Before the night was out, he and Catherine had exchanged their life stories and vowed to be partners. A partnership, as one writer was to put it later, of business and pleasure, as the two would meet after nightfall and scour the countryside for victims.

The ice-cool nerve which Catherine had already shown was tested to the full on the night of 10 June 1683, when one traveller the pair were robbing attempted to resist and she was forced to shoot him. Ironically, the very next day Lord Ferrers himself posted a reward of fifty pounds for anyone who could name the highwaymen responsible.

However, the secret smile which Lady Ferrers enjoyed on hearing this news was abruptly removed later in the day when her house steward informed her that he had seen her leaving the house at night and realized that she must be the mysterious highwayman. As he did not wish to see the family's good name besmirched, he would only agree to keep her secret from the master if she promised to stop her nefarious activities.

Realizing the danger she was in, Catherine agreed. Within the year the old man had died, taking her secret to the grave. In the interim, Jerry Jackson had been arrested and hung at Tyburn.

The need for excitement still bubbled in Lady Catherine Ferrer's blood, however, and once more, on a summer night in 1684, she took to the road. It was a foolish decision, for her luck had now run out – though quite how she met her fate has been a subject of disagreement, as one of her biographers, Margaret Pearson, has reported in *Bright Tapestry* (1956).

> Stories of what became of the lady vary considerably. Some say that she was shot, but that her horse took her home. She tried to reach a secret room she had prepared for such an emergency, staggering up a concealed staircase as the blood gushed out of her wounds. But she died on the stairs, and there her body was found. Other stories say she was caught red-handed and hanged.

Whichever account is true – and the hanging seems most unlikely because it is inconceivable that there would be no record of a member of the aristocracy going to the gallows – the story of Lady Ferrers is the stuff of romance and has deservedly inspired both a novel and two films.

The novel, which disguised Lady Ferrers under the name of Barbara Skelton was *The Life and Death of the Wicked Lady Skelton*, written by Magdalen King-Hall in 1944. The following year it formed the basis of the controversial Margaret Lockwood film, *The Wicked Lady*.

What created such a furore in the earlier movie was the amount of cleavage shown by Margaret Lockwood, which caused the picture to be banned in Birmingham (though only on Sundays), while, for showing in America, some forty close-ups of the star's ample bosom had to be cut. The movie still proved to be one of the most commercially successful pictures ever made in Britain, and Margaret Lockwood created a new role for British film heroines – they could be maddening as well as sexy. It was also the first British picture in which the heroine lived her life like a man: indulging in the pleasures of the flesh, taking to the roads as a highway robber and stooping to murder when found out. Though such a theme in these days of female liberation might seem tame, nothing quite like it had been seen before.

The British director, Michael Winner, remembers seeing *The Wicked Lady* ten times as a young man: 'In those days you never saw a low-cut gown so it was very daring'. Winner relished the chance to remake the story as a $15 million movie, shot on location in England. His version excited controversy because of a whip fight between Faye Dunaway and a bare-breasted young actress. An attempt to have the scene censored was resisted by Winner who, aided by a petition signed by fifty top film-industry people, got the decision reversed.

Today, interest in the story of the greatest of all the highwaywomen shows no sign of diminishing. Markyate Cell where she lived still exists, as does the secret passage she used for her night-time expeditions. And there is also a stain on the floor near the stairs which is believed to be Catherine's blood, spilled on returning from that fatal last mission. In the village nearby there is also an inn called the Wicked Lady, named after Lady Ferrers.

But, stranger still, her ghost is claimed to have been seen by local people riding in the fields and hills, and recently even appearing at a vicarage tea party! Michael Winner added to the legend by reporting having a strange experience while filming some scenes for the picture at Compton Wyniates, a stately home in Warwickshire. He had decided to use an old bedroom which was always kept locked and had not been used for years.

> It was weird. The camera went wrong, the lights went wrong, everything went wrong. We never did get any footage out of that room at all. Apparently the Wicked Lady haunts the house she used to live in in Hertfordshire. She must have popped over there as well!

Perhaps, though, Lady Ferrers is looking for the one thing her fame has always denied her – a final resting place. Because according to local stories, she lies buried in an unmarked grave in Hitchin ...

10 A Golden Era for Robbers?

The rapid series of changes on the English throne during the Jacobite era, and the ensuing more stable reigns of George I and his son, George II, had little effect on the nation's highwaymen. Villains from all walks of life continued to take to the roads in a rather dreary flood – many of them either army deserters or rural malcontents, not forgetting the petty thieves from the London slums – and for a time there seemed to be few new personalities of the ilk of Hind, Stafford or Duval to capture the public imagination.

Nor did any of these men appear to have the imagination to alter the now familiar highwayman's tactics, and they continued to prey on the same lonely traveller on horseback, or the occupants of an unguarded coach. Some, it is true, came into the towns and cities, and were not above operating in daylight: 'We are forced to travel, even at noon, as if we are going into battle', declared the writer, MP, and son of the famous Prime Minister, Horace Walpole, in a letter to some friends. (They were to prove words of astonishing foresight, for Walpole was himself later to be a victim of highwaymen!)

Although the numbers of highwaymen caught and hanged at Tyburn continued to rise during the first decades of the eighteenth century – in the 22-year period from 1749 to 1771, for example, 251 were swung – it was evident that a great many more were getting away scot-free. Indeed, it is probably true to say that highway robbery reached its peak at the middle of the century – a kind of 'golden era', according to some historians!

There were, of course, exceptions to the nonentities who clutter the court and assizes records of this period; and four men in particular stand head, shoulders, and even horses above the rest of the rabble. As their exploits were all celebrated in broadsheets, ballads, chapbooks, and newspaper reports, their fame can be discussed with accuracy more than two centuries later. The quartet are: 'Captain' James Whitney, "The Jacobite Robber", leader of one of the most daring bands of highwaymen of the time; William Parsons, the baronet's son who first practised highway robbery in America; another William, William Page, 'The Master of the Road', who meticulously planned his robberies and finally James Maclaine, 'The Ladies' Hero', who is believed to have inspired John Gay's famous work, *The Beggar's Opera*.

The title 'Captain' is deliberately put in quotes for James Whitney as his rank was self-awarded, although his good humour and the insistence with which he banned his men from using brutality in their hold-ups show him to have been a man in the same mould as the old Cavalier captains. Indeed, Whitney's biography, *The Jacobite Robber* (1693) refers specifically to his having inherited 'all the courage, boldness and dexterity of the famous Claude Du Vall and the Golden Farmer and the rest of his other noble predecessors'. (The title of this book has puzzled some historians, for the subject gave no sign of nursing a grudge against the House of Orange or of having wanted to further the cause of the pretender to the throne.)

James Whitney's origins, however, certainly did not suggest such a future, for he was said to have been born of 'mean, contemptible parentage' in 1660 in Stevenage, Hertfordshire and to have first been apprenticed to a butcher – shades of the infamous Dick Turpin! Curiously, some of the early reports of his robberies also name him 'Whitney the butcher highwayman'.

The meat trade apparently did not suit young James. His biography claims that he made an abortive trip to Essex to steal some calves, but was outwitted by a rascally owner and decided to quit the profession. In any event, he instead took over the running of the George Inn at Cheshunt in Hertfordshire, and was here introduced to the world of the highwaymen by some of his customers. Finding him a convivial and obliging host, a number of the men of the road tried to get him to join them. But why, he argued, should he become a highwayman when he could make good money behind the bar? As the author of *The Jacobite Robber* quaintly puts it:

> Whereas should he trade for himself the scour of the highways to the tune of 'Dammee, stand and deliver,' he must certainly at

> one time or another make a pilgrimage to Tyburn, and swinging in a rope he had a mortal aversion to, because his prophetical grandmother had formerly told him it was a dry sort of death.

But the glint of the many gold coins he saw in the hands of his customers – and an evident inclination to have some excitement and adventure away from the round-the-clock demands of an inn – finally changed his mind. Whitney sold up the George, bought an excellent horse, and went along with the others. His courage, quick wit and natural qualities of leadership soon made him the 'captain' of the group; and, though he had no practical experience of soldiering, he ran the band of men with all the efficiency of an army troop. Occasionally, though, he chose to ride alone and carried off solo hold-ups with equal success – his victims, be they men or women, finding him a gentleman and a gallant, according to *The Jacobite Robber.*

The book details a number of Whitney's robberies, of which we have space for only a few here. An early victim was a churchman from Greenwich, Mr Wawen, whom the gang held up on the outskirts of London. Having emptied the gentleman's pockets, Whitney declared that as it was so long since he had been to church, he demanded that the poor man should preach a sermon for him and his men.

Mr Wawen may well have been taken aback by this strange request, but he was evidently a man of humour himself for the text he took was THEFT:

> which being not to be divided into sentences nor syllables, as being but one word which is only a monosyllable, necessity therefore obliges me to divide into letters which I find to be five. Now T is Theological, H is Historical, E is Exegetical, F is Figurative and T is Tropological.

The minister then proceeded to elaborate on each letter, concluding:

> I desire that you will embrace this exhortation of St Paul the Apostle, 'Let him that stole steal no more,' or else the letters of my text point towards a tragical conclusion: for T, Take care; H, Hanging; E. Ends not; F, Felony; T, Tyburn.

If Mr Wawen had feared for his safety after such a diatribe against highway robbery he need not have worried. Whitney at once burst into laughter, and was joined by the others. So impressed was the captain by what he had heard, that he urged the men to take up a collection for the preacher.

A contemporary report concludes the story:

> So telling the money over which they had taken from him and finding it to be just ten pounds, they gave him ten shillings for his pains and then rode away to seek whom they might next devour.

In a later operation on his own on Bagshot Heath, Whitney was very nearly outsmarted by a traveller who declared, on being commanded to 'Stand and deliver!', that he, too, was a 'gentleman thief'. With a doff of his hat, the captain allowed the other to ride on – but that night, by pure chance, he happened to share the same inn as his intended victim and overheard him boasting to other travellers of how he had, to save a considerable sum of money, outsmarted a highwayman by pretending to be a robber himself.

The next morning, Whitney lay in wait for the man to quit the inn and once again levelled his pistols at him. When, for a second time, the man protested that he belonged to the brotherhood of the road, the captain was ready with a reply:

> Why, then, as it is an old saying that two of a trade can never agree, I must make bold to take what you have, wherefore deliver what you have instantly, or else I must be obliged to send a brace of balls through your head!

Realizing his bluff had been called, the man was forced to hand over his purse and Whitney, still smiling at his cleverness, rode away 120 guineas better off.

The Whitney gang carried out their trade in an area stretching from London to Doncaster, always striking quickly and moving on before pursuit could be organized. Regularly, they disbanded and went their own ways, to avoid appearing *en masse* in places where they might be recognized. As a later writer, Joseph Gollomb, remarked, Whitney was 'like Robin Hood all over again, with a dash of Captain Hind thrown in'.

On one famous occasion in the Midlands, when the gang held up a party which included one of the king's closest advisers, the captain enquired whether he and his men might be granted free pardons if they offered to leave the road and join the royal forces. There is no indication as to whether Whitney was being

Margaret Lockwood portraying the highwaywoman,
Lady Catherine Ferrers

Lady Catherine Ferrers as
played by Faye Dunaway

Another of the famous highwaywomen, Anne Holland, robbing
Dr Trotter in his home in Moorfields

William Parsons – the first highway robber in America! After learning his profession across the Atlantic, Parsons returned to London to terrorize English travellers

Jonathan Wild, the 'Thief–taker General', and a satirical invitation to his execution

The novelist, Henry Fielding who helped bring about the downfall of the highwaymen with his brother (*below*)

John Fielding, who became famous as the 'Blind Beak'

The great Cavalier highwayman,
John Clavel

'Cornered!' – a highwayman being arrested

A highwayman receiving friends and admirers in the condemned cell at Newgate

An example of the vast crowds which gathered at Tyburn for the executions of highwaymen

One of the last great characters of the road, 'Sixteen String Jack'

William 'Swift Nicks' Nevision, the highwayman who really made the legendary ride from London to York

The last highwayman, Robert Snooks, meets his end bravely

serious – presumably not, as he and his men cleared out the travellers of over £300 in cash!

The career of this latter-day Robin Hood came to a predictable end – but not without an unusual twist. Captain Alexander Smith has provided the details:

> Whitney was at length betrayed by one Madame Cosens, who kept a bawdy house in Milford Lane, and she had him apprehended in Whitefriars and sent to Newgate. Not long after his confinement being tried and condemned at the Old Bailey, he went with other malefactors to be executed at Tyburn. But in his journey thither a reprieve overtaking him, he was brought back again.

The reason for this reprieve was a promise the captain had apparently made to reveal a Jacobite plot, but he failed to convince anyone that it was genuine, and was again marked down for execution. He decided to die in the gentlemanly style he had adopted, and sent out for a richly embroidered suit and hat which cost £100. Smith concludes Whitney's story:

> Before he was taken to be hanged at Porters Block, by Smithfield, on Wednesday, December 19, 1694, he was still in great expectation of another reprieve, but came the day and all hopes of another respite having passed, he confessed his condemnation was just, and after several minutes for private devotion, he was tumbled out of this world into another, when about 34 years of age.

William Parsons, our next highwayman, had no need to pretend to be a gentleman, for he was the youngest son of a Nottinghamshire baronet, the nephew of the Duchess of Northumberland. His is a story of profligacy turning to criminality.

Parsons was born in 1717, and had a first-class education at Eton purchased for him. He fell, however, to the temptation – as did many rich men's sons – of the card school. To pay his debts he not only stole from his schoolfellows, but also from his family, including his aunt, the duchess. His despairing father tried to cure this passion by sending the boy to sea as a midshipman on board HMS *Romney* cruising to the West Indies; but when he was caught cheating at cards he was forced to leave the service. Another scheme for him to work in an administrative job in the Royal African Company in West Africa was no more successful.

There followed a marriage, in 1740, to a young girl with a dowry of £12,000, which soon ended in disaster when he squandered the money at the gambling tables. Once again, his long suffering family came to William's aid by purchasing him a commission in the Army, but his gambling compulsion lead him deeper into trouble and he began to forge warrants for money. He was arrested, tried at Maidstone assizes in 1745, and sentenced to transportation to a Virginia slave plantation: the kind of sentence only a baronet's son with connections might have escaped with, for in those days forgery was a hanging crime.

Unfortunately, the records of William Parsons's time in America are rather incomplete, but there is strong evidence that he became a highway robber – one of the first to be seen in the New World, which, of course, a little later on was to be beset by mounted gunmen of all sorts in the old 'Wild West'. Charles Harper has perhaps the most detailed résumé of this part of Parson's career:

> Working in the plantation belonging to Lord Fairfax, he attracted the attention of that nobleman, who took him from the gang of convicted malefactors, with whom, under strict supervision, he hoed and delved under the blazing sun, and befriended him. It did not pay to befriend William Parsons. He stole one of the best horses belonging to his benefactor, and, going upon those early colonial roads, soon accumulated as a highwayman, a sufficient sum to buy himself a passage back to England.

It should come as a surprise to no one that, having at last succeeded in an undertaking, William Parsons decided to continue his career of robbery on the roads of England.

Parsons worked as a loner throughout the western suburbs of London – in particular between Turnham Green and Hounslow Heath – and, though he is credited with some extensive hauls from the coaches of gentlefolk rather less than his equal in social terms, he was unable to resist his compulsion to gamble with the proceeds, and soon had to return for more. The facts that he chose not to wear a mask, and appeared too often in the same locality, were to be his downfall.

According to a pamphlet published just after his death, *The Baronet's Son: Being a Discovery of the Crimes and Forgeries of William Parsons*, he obtained information that a servant with a valise containing a large sum of money was to leave town and meet his master in Windsor. He set out to lie in wait for him.

> But he had already been so active upon the Heath that his face was well known and he was recognised at Brentford by a traveller who had suffered at his hands before. Following him into Hounslow Town, this former victim suddenly raised the alarm and caused him to be seized. Taken to the Rose and Crown Inn, Parsons was recognised by the landlord and others as one who had for some time scoured the Heath and committed robberies. His pistols were taken from him and he was committed to Newgate.

The baronet's son was tried and convicted and, despite desperate appeals by himself and his family, there was to be no escape from justice this time. He was taken out to Tyburn and swung on 11 February 1751 – aged thirty-four.

The third highwayman of this so called 'golden era', William Page, was also something of a strategist, like 'Captain' James Whitney, but he was a serious planner, too, and probably no other highwayman matched him for the care and attention to detail which he put into all his hold-ups.

Page spent countless hours familiarizing himself with the layout of London and its outskirts, drawing detailed maps of every major and minor road within twenty miles of the capital, and then thoroughly acquainting himself with an area in which he planned to rob. He would also pick out the best spot for an ambush and make sure he knew the quickest way to make a getaway with his spoils. Nor did Page's ingenuity end there, for he also introduced 'some interesting novelties into the well-worn business', according to one of his biographers, Arthur Griffiths.

> He travelled always in a phaeton and pair driven by a confederate, and in this respectable conveyance his real character was not suspected. He used to dress in a lace or embroidered frock and wear his hair tied behind. When he had been driven a distance from London he would turn into some infrequented place, and having disguised himself in other clothes, with a grizzle or black wig, would saddle one of the

> carriage horses, and, riding to the main road, commit a robbery. This done, he hastened back to the carriage, resumed his usual dress, and drove back to London. He was frequently cautioned to be on his guard against one particularly daring highwayman (himself) who might meet and rob him. 'No, no,' Page would reply, 'he cannot do it a second time, unless he robs me of my coat and shirt, for he has taken all my money already!

For a man who had such grand ideas, William Page was humbly born in 1730, the son of a bargeman who worked for a coal merchant at Hampton on the Thames. William's father died when the boy was ten, and, although his mother raised him as best she could, he fell victim to a terrible vanity. Apprenticed to a haberdasher in his mid-teens he became – in the words of Christopher Hibbert – 'a consummate coxcomb perpetually employing tailors to alter his clothes to any new fashion he had seen'.

The cost of this vanity lead William to steal from his employers. On the discovery of this, he was lucky to be dismissed rather than handed over to the authorities. With no references, he was forced to take a much more menial job as a livery-servant to a certain Captain Jasper. This resulted in the young man unintentionally confronting his destiny – for while on a journey with his master, their coach was held up and the boy watched goggle-eyed as more money than he had ever seen before was handed over to the mounted man behind a pistol.

William vowed to take to the road himself and, borrowing a horse and some pistols, held up his first traveller on Highgate Hill. His haul was only four pounds, but it was a start. Emboldened, he next tackled the Canterbury stagecoach on Shooters Hill and took over thirty pounds. A third foray on Hounslow Heath provided an even larger purse – and no little amusement. For the man he stopped with a wave of his pistol and from whom he took almost £100 in money and valuables was none other than his former employer, Captain Jasper!

It may have been the novelty of this situation – or the realization that he might have been recognized – that made William Page decide that successful highway robbery could be guaranteed only by careful planning. It was several months, in fact, before 'The Master of the Road', as he was to become known, ventured back on the highway with his carefully prepared maps, and open carriage, to deceive other travellers.

Page's biographers tell us that the use of this phaeton once nearly backfired on him. For, after committing a hold-up on a road near Putney, he returned to where he had left the carriage, only to find it gone. As he was still in disguise and on horseback, his plans would be ruined unless he could find it.

The master planner was not to be easily beaten, however, and set off in pursuit of his missing carriage, following the clearly visible tracks along the road. He found it parked outside an inn where it had been taken by a party of haymakers who had assumed it had been abandoned. But how to recover it without giving the game away?

Again, Page had a brain-wave. Stripping down to his underwear, he threw his highwayman's clothes into a well and went up to the inn. Stumbling through the doorway, the dishevelled figure claimed he had been pounced upon and robbed by some highwaymen who had also taken his carriage. Pointing an accusing finger at the simple countrymen, Page had no difficulty in convincing the landlord that they must be the miscreants and that – despite their protests – he should call the authorities.

Although the haymakers were arrested and Page recovered his phaeton, he did the decent thing by refusing to give evidence against them; because, he said, he had recovered his property and had been done no real harm. The men were consequently released. Page, though, realized the mishap could easily happen again and decided to use the conveyance just for joy-rides and to rob only on horseback.

The next three years of William Page's life satisfied all his desires. He is said to have planned and committed something like three hundred successful robberies (a number in company with a new accomplice named John Darwell, whom he had known since childhood). He appeased his vanity with expensive clothes and trips to fashionable provincial resorts such as Bath, Tunbridge, Newmarket and Scarborough. Like William Parsons, though, Page could not resist the gaming tables and, as one report says, 'all he made by pillage he lost at play'.

It was a robbery on Blackheath in 1757, when he and Darwell confronted a formidable soldier named Captain Farrington, that led to the end of the great planner's career. Among the items Darwell took from the captain was a gold repeater watch with which he could not bring himself to part.

Immediately after the robbery, Captain Farrington organized a search-party to try and capture the men, but they eluded their pursuers by taking a ferry across the Thames to Twickenham. All was not lost for the captain, however. When Darwell carried out an ill-conceived hold-up of his own on a coach at Sevenoaks, it turned out to contain five men armed with pistols. He was captured and the repeater watch was found on him. In an attempt to save himself, Darwell turned King's evidence and implicated his former school-friend in the robbery of Captain Farrington. Two weeks later, William Page was arrested in one of his old haunts in London – the Golden Lion in Grosvenor Square – and clapped into Newgate.

The man who had brought a new dimension into highway robbery suffered the same fate as all the rest when he was tried, sentenced, and executed on 6 April 1758.

The last of the quartet of highwaymen, James Maclaine (sometimes spelled Maclean), 'The Ladies' Hero', was as famous in his century as Claude Duval had been in the previous one. His successes as a robber – after an inauspicious beginning – plus his conquests of society women were very nearly the equal of the Frenchman's, although he was perhaps more of a gentleman, being very discreet about the names of the ladies he bedded. Not for nothing was he called 'The Gentleman Highwayman' during his lifetime – although the fact remains (and portraits prove it) that he was a tall, rather gangling man with staring, fish-like eyes and a pock-marked face.

Maclaine was certainly not born a gentleman: his father, Laughlin Maclaine, was a Scottish Presbyterian minister who had settled in the little Irish town of Monaghan, where his son was born in 1724. The boy was well educated, proving himself adept at writing and accounts, and his father intended him to go into business with a Scottish merchant in Rotterdam. However, just before James's eighteenth birthday, the old minister died and left the young man enough money to ensure that work was not an immediate requisite. Squandering his inheritance in less than a year, though, James was forced to work briefly as a butler for a man in Cork before deciding that the money and conditions could not pay for the life-style to which he aspired: so he set off for London.

The young Irishman was dazzled by the fine clothes of the gentlemen and the inviting eyes of the fast women of the city, and he set about obtaining both. His charming manners and smooth tongue soon secured him a bride with a dowry of £500. Neither lasted very long, however – by 1748 the money had been lost in a chandler's business, and his wife had died of small pox. Still, he yearned to be a gentleman of fortune and to taste more of the delights of London life – in particular the female life, high as well as low. Maclaine found the solution to his dilemma while discussing his situation with William Plunkett, a chemist who had shared adjacent premises to his and was now, like him, bankrupt.

According to a pamphlet published about Maclaine this is how Plunkett convinced his friend of their destiny:

> 'A brave man cannot want. He has a right to live, and need not want the conveniences of life. While the dull, plodding, busy knaves carry cash in their pockets, we must draw upon them to supply our wants. Only impudence is necessary, and getting the better of a few idle scruples. Courage is scarcely necessary, for all we have to deal with are mere poltroons.'

These were brave words, and, though Plunkett may have convinced himself, Maclaine made a nervous, almost frightened, highwayman to begin with. Despite being well armed and wearing a 'Venetian masque' that completely hid his face, his courage failed him when the pair held up a lone grazier on his way home from Smithfield. It was Plunkett who had to make the demands and extract the sixty pounds from their victim.

James was not a lot better when the pair decided to hold up a coach on the road to St Albans. It was agreed that Maclaine would halt the coach with his pistols and Plunkett would ride up to take the valuables. But, according to a biography written after his death, 'he several times rode up intending to make the challenge, but each time fell back unable to speak'. Once again his associate had to take over before the two men could make off with over £100 in jewellery and cash.

Plunkett, though, continued to goad his partner on with, it seems, some success. A broadsheet reports:

> During the next six months they had committed alone or together some sixteen robberies in Hyde Park, near Marylebone, or within 20 miles of London, and got some large prizes. They rode down towards Chester, too, and waylaid several persons

> between Stony Stratford and Whitechurch, but their greatest haul was after their return to town, when, hearing that an officer of the East India Company's services was bringing a large sum of money to London, they stopped him near Greenwich.

But if Maclaine was not an outstanding highwayman to begin with, he more than made up for this with the ladies. He used his share of the spoils to take rooms in St James's Street and pass himself off as an Irish squire, dressing colourfully in a crimson suit, a silk waistcoat with lace trimmings, black velvet breeches and yellow morocco slippers! An ever-increasing number of women began to fall at the feet of this smooth-talking gentleman of town whose dark eyes seemed to hint at deep passions and secret adventures ...

The episode that made James Maclaine famous, however, was an encounter with Horace Walpole in Hyde Park. The great man was returning from Kensington to his London home on a moonlit night in 1749 when Maclaine and Plunkett stopped his carriage. Walpole had a narrow escape from death when Maclaine's pistol went off, apparently accidentally, and a bullet grazed the skin under his eye, leaving some shot marks on his face and completely stunning him.

Writing later of the incident, Walpole rather startled his readers by declaring that 'the whole affair was conducted with the greatest good breeding on both sides'. He further revealed that the following morning he had received from Maclaine 'two letters of excuses, which, with less wit than the epistles of Voltaire, had ten times more natural and easy politeness in the turn of their expression'. Maclaine, he added, said that 'had the bullet found its billet in your head, I would certainly have put one through my own'.

In a wry postscript to the second letter, Maclaine apparently offered to return any items that he had taken from Walpole of which he was particularly fond! These could be secured 'for a small price', and the highwayman suggested they might meet to conduct this business one midnight at Tyburn!

Fanned by Walpole's love of gossip this story of 'The Gentleman Highwayman' was soon the talk of London. The man himself pressed home the advantage by appearing wherever fashionable society gathered, all the while hoping he might find a wealthy bride and no longer need to resort to arms to pay his way. In the interim, he continued to accept the favours of other ladies – both married and single – who found him irresistible.

The alliance of Maclaine and Plunkett finally came to an abrupt end on 26 June 1750. At two o'clock in the morning, the pair held up the Salisbury coach on Turnham Green, and there robbed five men and one woman 'who gave not the least show of resistance', according to a later report. It was a different story, however, when the highwaymen soon afterwards encountered another coach in which the Earl of Eglinton was travelling with two mounted servants.

Maclaine, who was now much bolder, rode up and instructed the driver to halt. It was actually a braver move than might at first have seemed evident, for the earl was known to carry a blunderbuss with him whenever he travelled. Plunkett was coming up from the rear and was able to disarm the nobleman as soon as the earl thrust the weapon through the coach window to open fire. Without a thought to the possible consequences, Maclaine decided to take the blunderbuss as a souvenir. The hold-up had been a close shave, and both men must have ridden off into the night with a sense of relief as well as their booty.

Maclaine, however, compounded his foolishness when he returned to St James's Street, for, a little later, he called a dealer to his rooms and offered to sell a number of the items he had taken from the earl's coach, including the blunderbuss. It can only be assumed that he was in dire need of money. And when this item was recognized as was inevitable, and the sale traced back to Maclaine, 'The Gentleman Highwayman' found himself in the dock of the Old Bailey. Plunkett, learning of what had happened to his partner, fled London and was never heard of again.

Though Maclaine made a spirited defence – calling no fewer than nine witnesses to testify to his character, including Lady Caroline Petersham who told the bench: 'I have had the pleasure to know him well; he has often been about my house and I never lost anything' – he was found guilty of robbery and sentenced to hang at Tyburn. The case naturally caused a sensation, not least because of the numbers of ladies who had professed to know Maclaine, as good as confessing their intimacies with him.

Horace Walpole, who had understandably followed the trial with great interest, wrote in the immediate aftermath:

> As I conclude he will suffer, and wish him no ill, I don't care to have his idea, and am almost single in not having been to see him ... But the chief personages who have been to comfort and weep over this fallen hero are Lady Caroline Petersham and Miss Ashe: I call them Polly and Lucy and asked them if he did not sing, 'Thus I stand like the Turk with his doxies around'.

Those who are familiar with John Gay's famous musical play, *The Beggar's Opera* – which had just then been produced in London to enormous acclaim – will immediately spot the allusion to its final song in Walpole's reference; and will doubtless also know that Polly and Lucy were the two girlfriends of the highwayman hero of the show, Captain Macheath. Though Gay never said specifically that James Maclaine was his source of inspiration, few doubted it then and even fewer do today.

Maclaine's celebrity brought thousands clamouring to Newgate for a last glimpse of him before the hangman did his work on 3 October. Outside the prison, hawkers did a roaring trade with a broadsheet entitled *Newgate's Lamentation, or the Ladies' Last Farewell of Maclaine*, two verses of which will provide the flavour of the whole:

> Farewell, my friends, let not your hearts be filled,
> My time is near, and I'll with calmness yield.
> Fair ladies now, your grief, I pray, forbear,
> Nor wound me with each tender-hearted tear.
>
> Mourn not my fate; your friendships have been kind,
> Which I in tears shall own, till breath's resigned.
> Oh! may the indulgence of such friendly love,
> That's been bestowed on me, be doubled from above.

It is not, in fact, just James Maclaine's time that was near; something else far more significant was about to pass into history. Not only was the last of the highwaymen of the 'golden era' going to meet his maker, but the very occupation which he had followed was also to end.

Indeed, a number of the people who were primarily

responsible for bringing about this finale were standing on the edge of the crowd as Maclaine stepped into eternity. Some of them may well have begun to realize that *their* time had come. For, in truth, a new era was dawning – the era of 'The Thief-takers'.

11 The Coming of the Thief-takers

It is one of the strangest facts in the history of highwaymen that not only did the English people resist for generations the establishment of a professional police-force who might have protected them against highway robbery but the man who did finally initiate the decline in their numbers, the notorious Jonathan Wild, had actually been intimately associated with them before becoming a thief-taker.

Although it might be concluded from the number of them who were caught and hanged during the eighteenth and nineteenth centuries, that the pursuit of highwaymen was well organized, the truth is that we only have the details of those who met their fate at Tyburn from which to draw such conclusions. There were undoubtedly a great many more who escaped capture, retired on the proceeds of their crimes, or just faded away with age: none of them leaving so much as a line for us to study in any assizes register or newspaper report.

As the previous chapters have shown, during the first half of the eighteenth century, the so-called 'golden era', highwaymen were better armed and organized than ever before, and carried off their loot almost at will. No matter what the careful traveller tried to do to ensure a safe journey, he or she was constantly at risk by day or night on the roads radiating from London to the four corners of the country. Complaints to parliament about this state of affairs fell on deaf ears: it was still the responsibility of the hundreds (divisions of the various counties) to administer the law in their districts. Occasionally, as we have seen, soldiers were called out to deal with particularly violent gangs, and wealthy victims sometimes posted their own rewards for the capture of highwaymen. But successive governments had formulated no specific policy for dealing with the menace of the highwaymen.

Such machinery for upholding the law as there was consisted of constables appointed by the local authorities from ordinary citizens, in much the same way as men and women are selected to appear on juries today. It was clearly a highly unsatisfactory arrangement, for the duty of a constable was obligatory, unpaid (until 1792), and the term of office was for one year. There were no special qualifications for the job, and, as the constable had to continue to earn his living whilst carrying out his duties, the time and dedication he might be able to give to the unenviable task would be extremely limited. Not surprisingly, then, the quality of constables was low, and the only highwayman likely to fall into their hands was a sleeping or drunken one who had been informed upon!

Some richer members of the general public employed their own guards to protect them on journeys, whilst wealthy householders in cities like London hired watchmen to look out for the villains who might accost them or break into their homes at night. But, again, the indications are that it was mostly older men unable to get work in more demanding occupations who filled these posts.

Though this system of law obviously cried out for change, the English people seemed determinedly opposed to the idea of a professional police-force. The civil war which had brought the Puritans to power was still firmly entrenched in the public mind, and there was a fear of the return of tyranny mixed with a devotion to the concept of freedom as it was then perceived. The people of the nation dreaded change: and they saw in the establishment of the kind of police-forces which were then being created in Europe a very real threat to individual liberty.

It is said that the mere mention of the word police – a French word not to come into usage until 1714 – caused great unease. There were those who argued powerfully that the cost of establishing a police-force would ruin the economy. Indeed, the loss of money and valuables – by people who could generally afford such things at the hands of these highwaymen – was held to be more acceptable than spending much larger sums to prevent the crimes. In a nutshell, the English clung to the idea that the old ways were the best ways: the people themselves should look after their own and be responsible for bringing criminals to justice.

The highwayman's unhampered freedom on England's roads

was, however, finally brought to an end by three main factors – according to the Norfolk-born traveller and social historian George Borrow, reporting after one of his lengthy journeys about the countryside, in his book *Romany Rye* (1857):

> The refusal to licence public houses that were known to afford shelter to highwaymen, the enclosure of many wild heaths in the country, and particularly the establishing in the neighbourhood of London of a well-armed mounted patrol.

These changes were not easily effected, however – nor brought about without the activities of some very dissimilar people.

The story might fairly be said to begin with Jonathan Wild, who is listed in most national biographies as 'The Thief-taker', though he was just as famous in his time as the boss of London's criminal underworld which he ran on a combination of fear and paid informants.

Although the legal concept of the common informer had been in operation for close on a thousand years, it was not until the reign of William and Mary (1688–1702) that a system of rewards for information was given a legal basis by an act that offered forty pounds for the conviction of a highwayman. The informant was also promised the property of the highwayman – including his horse and pistols – and a pardon for his own crimes if he happened to be of the same profession! At a stroke this decree gave rise to a new profession, thief-taking, and it was Wild who demonstrated just how profitable it might be. Indeed, it was not without justification that the novelist Henry Fielding, who was also to be involved in the war against the highwaymen, referred to him as 'Jonathan Wild the Great' for, during his career, the lives – and deaths – of many of the country's criminals, including highwaymen, lay solely in his hands.

Wild was born in 1683, the son of a hard-working Wolverhampton wig-maker, who appears to have taken little interest in the boy, or his younger brother, for both led undisciplined childhoods and turned to crime in manhood. Jonathan was apprenticed at the age of fifteen to a buckle-maker in Birmingham, and, while still serving his indenture, married, and fathered a son. However, at twenty-one the lack of excitement caused Wild to desert his family and head for London where he lived in 'an orgy of pleasure and gaiety', to quote from *Jonathan Wild – Prince of Robbers* (1936) by Frederick J. Lyons. Until, that is, he fell into debt and was imprisoned in Wood Street Compter.

Although Wild had to serve four years in the prison, he put the time to good use and learned everything he could about the London criminal underworld. One of his teachers, the *Newgate Calendar* states, was a prostitute named Mary Milliner, with whom he formed 'a close familiarity'. The pair went into business on their release. It proved a mutually satisfying partnership, for, after Jonathan had worked as Mary's pimp for a year, the couple had made enough money to set up a brothel in Lewkenors Lane.

Jonathan had his sights set on higher things, however. One of the facts that had remained most clear in his mind from his days of imprisonment was how much money there was to be made by handling stolen property – in particular the booty of highwaymen. Shortly afterwards he opened another brothel in Cripplegate which was merely to serve as a front for his activities as a fence.

The business that Jonathan Wild created was in fact little different to the one that had been pioneered by Moll Cutpurse. First, he made it known to highwaymen and other members of the criminal fraternity that he would buy the proceeds of their robberies; secondly, he placed advertisements to let gentlemen and ladies who had had items of jewellery stolen that they might well get them returned – for a price – if they contacted him. He had, he said, the contacts among the criminal classes: but he would charge a consultation fee of five shillings and approximately half the market-value of the goods returned.

Not surprisingly, the business prospered mightily, and Jonathan's ambitions soared still higher. He soon became the central figure in the stolen-property market, but wanted to be something more: the ruler of the criminal underworld. The man who was to help him achieve this ambition was Charles Hitchin, a homosexual city marshall, who used his office to line his pockets and his power to influence justice.

Wild and Hitchin made a formidable team for a while, but it was Jonathan who gained the greater benefit, adding knowledge of the law and the city marshal's skill at arresting thieves to his criminal insight. He had, though, no compunction in deserting Hitchin when the official was finally exposed and dismissed from his post. Wild now saw himself as a prince amongst London thieves and began to exert his knowledge and power to build up a criminal fraternity of shop-lifters, house-breakers, footpads, pick-pockets and, of course, highwaymen. All owed him their allegiance and soon learned that they crossed him at their peril.

Even the briefest examination of Wild's life reveals that he had a brilliant gift for organization. He first divided London and the suburbs into different areas, each worked by separate gangs under his central control. Then he moved his specialized criminals to wherever they might get the richest pickings, and set up an information service – of particular value to highwaymen – supplying details of the movements of wealthy travellers. He himself took to having a personal bodyguard, probably the first 'gangster' in history to do so. The Mafia 'families' of modern times could have taught Jonathan Wild nothing about making crime big business!

Still Jonathan was not content – but then he had the brain-wave which was to change his life, and, equally, the history of highway robbery. He would use his inside knowledge of crime and criminals to become the 'Thief-taker General of Great Britain and Ireland', as he decided to call himself. It was a scheme that, right from the outset, could hardly fail.

On the one hand, Wild could present himself to the world as a public spirited 'private detective' bringing criminals to justice; and on the other, he could use his office to enforce discipline among his own gangs by getting those who tried to work outside his circle arrested – and threatening the same to anyone who defied his authority. It soon became evident that no one Wild brought to court was likely to be acquitted, and the authorities also began to seek his assistance in the battle against crime. The 'Thief-taker General' now had both the robbers and the robbed at his beck and call.

A later report says:

> As a thief taker he was audacious and brilliant. He had one man hanged in order to sleep with his widow. If anyone threatened to expose him, Wild immediately brought a capital charge against the man, fabricating enough evidence for conviction of a felony; for as the law stood, no felon could give evidence against anyone else.

Wild also set himself up in a new house near the Old Bailey – a kind of symbol, to all those who came to do business with him, of the double power he wielded – and he mischievously sometimes entertained civic dignitaries at the same table as highwaymen. Another symbol of his position as the uncrowned King of the Underworld was a silver staff he carried with a small crown mounted on the top.

Quite how many convictions 'The Thief-taker' secured has never been accurately estimated, although in an audacious and ultimately unsuccessful petition he sent to the Lord Mayor of London – to try and have the seal set on his climb in society by being made a freeman – he claimed to have sent over sixty criminals to the gallows. Many of these were certainly highwaymen, for their natural tendency to independence and dislike of organization would have made them the one group of criminals over whom Wild would have had the greatest difficulty exerting his authority.

But Wild's pretence of being a public benefactor, coupled with his abuse of power, was beginning to make him enemies, in particular the recorder of London, Sir William Thompson, who became Solicitor-General in 1717 and brought in a bill making it a capital felony to take a reward under the pretence of helping the owner to recover his stolen goods. But the ingenious Jonathan soon found a way round this setback to his schemes – which actually became known in common parlance as 'Jonathan Wild's Act' – by abolishing his five shilling consultation fee and calling his place of business an enquiry office! After this his prosperity continued unabated, and such were the number of items that came into his office that he soon established another branch office, and even began shipping articles across the Channel for sale in Ostend.

In 1724, however, after almost fifteen years of absolute rule, the storm-clouds began to gather over Wild's empire. And it was not to be the law that would bring 'The Thief-taker' down, but two of his own men. One was Jack Sheppard, a house-breaker, who became famous for a number of daring escapes from prison; and the other was Joseph Blake, also a house-breaker and occasional highwayman better known by the nickname 'Blueskin', after his very dark complexion. These two had made a successful pair of robbers and decided that, instead of lining Wild's pockets still further, they would sell the proceeds of their robberies to another small-time fence named William Field who offered much better prices. When Wild found out what was happening he vowed vengeance and had little difficulty in getting both Sheppard and 'Blueskin' arrested on trumped-up charges.

Wild himself stage-managed the trial of the two men at the Old Bailey and had them duly condemned to death. Still preening himself with satisfaction, though, he visited Joseph Blake in his prison cell – and very nearly paid for this display of vanity with his life. For 'Blueskin', pretending that he wanted to whisper something in his former chief's ear, instead pulled out a knife and slit the man's throat 'from ear to ear'.

At first it was rumoured that Wild had died, and even before this was confirmed Dean Swift wrote a satirical elegy entitled 'Blueskin's Ballad' which delighted Londoners. But the news was premature: Wild recovered and it was Blake who went to meet his maker on the gallows. Jack Sheppard, however, was not finished with, and went on to achieve great notoriety by twice escaping from Newgate prison whilst awaiting execution. But he was seemingly quite unable to resist enjoying the celebrity this unique achievement bestowed upon him, and, while travelling openly across Finchley Common, was seized for a third time. This time he was not left alone for a moment until he was due to ride to Tyburn. A huge and admiring crowd, including many tearful females, witnessed his death, aged just twenty-two.

The die against Jonathan Wild had, however, been cast, and in 1725 he was arrested himself for procuring the return of some stolen lace. By a real piece of irony he had fallen into a trap of his own making – and the fact was not lost upon the trial judge, none other than Sir William Thompson, who must have taken a quiet satisfaction at seeing his 1718 act finally bring down the man who had inspired it. Wild, though, pleaded his case brilliantly, claiming that he had now brought a total of seventy-six criminals to justice (although some authorities give 120 as a more likely total); but the case was watertight. He was sentenced to the gallows and, according to one report of the time, 'there was great rejoicing in the Underworld which Wild had ruled for so long and so much to his own benefit'.

It was a significant moment in legal history, too – for henceforth a criminal had only the authorities to fear; he could sell his wares to whomever he chose.

Wild had one last card to play – he tried to cheat the huge

crowds who were gathering to see him swing on 24 May 1725 by taking an overdose of laudanum. But he did not die and was pronounced fit enough to ride to Tyburn, suffering the indignity of being pelted with mud and stones all the way. There were, undoubtedly, many amongst those hurling missiles who had lived in fear of 'The Thief-taker' and now savoured every sweet moment of his humiliation.

But despite Wild's inglorious end, the profession of thief-taking, which he had instituted, was by now growing and even taking on an aura of public respectability. The government had become impressed by the number of robbers who had been brought to justice by paid informers, and in turn added to the list of felonies which carried a reward for their disclosure.

However, as the system became more complex and anomalies arose over the 'value' of felons, the possibilities for corruption which Jonathan Wild had so successfully exploited were adopted by other, less able criminals. Now, with an army deserter being worth a mere pound to a thief-taker, with a horse-thief fetching ten pounds and a highwayman topping the list at forty pounds, one is not surprised to learn that some of Wild's progeny actually encouraged the criminal classes to aspire to better types of crime.

Some thief-takers, it is said, even sponsored young men to become highway robbers, obtaining horses, weapons and disguises for them. Once these dupes had committed a hold-up, they would arrange for their arrest and then pocket the reward. It is difficult to imagine even desperate young men falling for such a ploy, but the eighteenth century was very different from our own, with starvation a real threat to the lives of many poor people who had precious little alternative but to risk everything for a few decent meals.

Under such circumstances, it is no wonder the reward system continued to flourish even when thinking men drew attention to its inadequacies and showed how it was the innocent who became its victims. A look at parliamentary figures indicates that increasingly large sums of money were being paid out every year to the thief-takers: in 1736, for example, the total was £10,000; a year later, £15,000. Curiously, such expenditure was greeted by MPs as demonstrating the efficaciousness of the system, while the much smaller amounts spent on trying to prevent crime were sharply criticized.

It was to two men that the public came to owe an undying debt of gratitude for setting up a more satisfactory method of crime prevention in the middle years of the century: the novelist, Henry Fielding, now best remembered as the author of that great 'comic-epic' *Tom Jones* (1749); and his half-brother, John, who, though he had been completely blind since an accident in his youth, saw justice more clearly than almost any man of perfect sight.

Despite his continuing fame as a novelist, Henry Fielding also deserves recognition for two other achievements. First, by ridiculing the Prime Minister on stage in his popular burlesques, *Pasquin* (1736) and *The Historical Register* (1737), he provoked for good or ill the Licensing Act of 1737 under which the Lord Chamberlain was empowered to censor all plays. Secondly, out of necessity he took the job of principal magistrate at Bow Street and in this office helped to create what is now the British police-force.

This remarkable man was born in Glastonbury in 1707, the son of an Army general. After a literary education at Eton and in Leyden, he became an author-manager in London until the lampoon of the PM in 1737 closed his theatre. Forced to find an alternative means of earning his living he turned, maybe understandably, to the law, and, although he continued to write novels such as *Joseph Andrews* (1742) and an ironic history of *Jonathan Wild* (1743), financial stability eluded him. Five years on, and still short of work, he chose to follow in Wild's footsteps – though with very different and wholly honourable motives.

It was in October 1748 that Fielding was appointed Commissioner of the Peace for Middlesex (and later Westminster), taking up an office in Bow Street that had been occupied previously by one Colonel Thomas de Veil. De Veil had served in the job since 1729, and, though he had started the war against crime and done some exemplary detective work, there was an unsavoury side to him that worried many people. He was a crude, vulgar and extravagant man with a lust for women, and apparently kept in his office at Bow Street what he called 'a private closet for the examination of the fair sex'. Beyond the confines of this closet he also married four times and fathered twenty-five children!

De Veil certainly enjoyed a good life style as a 'trading justice', although he undoubtedly broke up a number of the criminal gangs of London, while in the process making Bow Street the most important magistrates court in England. At the end of his career he was able to claim, with some justification, to have executed or transported over 1,900 of the 'greatest malefactors that ever appeared in England'.

When Henry Fielding succeeded de Veil, he had no specific ideas of reform in his mind beyond continuing the fight against crime. But, as a more imaginative and less self-seeking officer, he was to prove the right man for the job at just the right time.

Fielding's post as a magistrate was unpaid, although the 'perks' were reckoned to be worth £1,000 per year. Though there is no doubt that Henry was keen to improve his financial lot, the fact remains that he did his job both honestly and humanely and still reduced this figure to about £300, a large proportion of which he had to pay his clerk. And, for someone who had been a disgruntled and disillusioned dramatist, he set about his work with surprising enthusiasm and dedication.

Fielding's first objective was a thorough examination of the eighty or so constables who were then the law's sole custodians on the streets and highways of London. It did not take him long to learn that many of them were corrupt or inefficient and that even the best had to do their duties after a hard day's work. Many, not surprisingly, left the service at the end of twelve months. The limitations of all of them were obvious, but he decided to keep a number under observation and, at the end of the year, urged a group of six constables he felt he could trust, to stay on in their posts. There was no salary he could offer them, merely the prompt payment of any thief-taker's reward they might claim.

Fired by Fielding's own enthusiasm, however, these men took to their tasks with a will and under their chief's guidance began to make inroads into the vast world of crime. In time, others were recruited to their ranks, and the force, not surprisingly, began to be known as 'Mr Fielding's People'. Later, they would be still better known as the Bow Street Runners.

Within two years, Fielding had some eighty men covering London, and, though the public were becoming aware of their growing efficiency, the chief also employed his pen to make sure the point was being driven home, giving statements to the press and inserting advertisements, such as this one in the *General Advertiser* of 5 February 1750: 'Near forty highwaymen, street robbers, burglars, rogues, vagabonds and cheats have been committed within a week by Justice Fielding'.

Armed with the evidence of his achievements, Fielding now urged the government to finance a professional police-force. And had parliament not stubbornly refused to do so almost solely on the grounds of cost, there can be little doubt that the novelist turned thief-taker would have anticipated Sir Robert Peel and his 'Peelers' by almost seventy-five years.

But Fielding was not a man to be easily beaten and in 1751, more than ever convinced that the prevention of crime was of greater importance than the catching of criminals, he attempted to win public support – and through it parliamentary backing – by publishing a pamphlet entitled *An Enquiry into the Causes of the Late Increase of Robberies, with some Proposals for Remedying this Growing Evil.* Curiously, this work is often ignored by Fielding's biographers, and though some of its findings seem negative and even repressive, it was to have a tremendous effect on the history of crime prevention.

One major effect was to prod the government into bringing in two important bills which became law the following year. The first was the Gin Act which restricted the sale of gin to licensed premises, and the second, an 'Act for Better Preventing Thefts and Robberies', which took Sir William Thompson's 1718 act to its logical conclusion, making the receiving of any property known to be stolen (as well as advertising for stolen property) a criminal offence. The ghost of Jonathan Wild was now well and truly laid.

In 1751, under mounting pressure of work, Fielding recruited his half-brother John as his assistant, and those who might have wondered at the appointment of a blind man to the post soon learned that he was possessed of the most remarkable hearing and instinct. Indeed it was later claimed that he could recognize 3,000 thieves by their voices alone. To further the battle against crime, Henry also launched a periodical called the *Covent Garden Journal* in which he sought even greater co-operation from the general public, as a typical statement from an issue in 1752 reveals:

> All persons who shall in the future suffer by highwaymen, robbers, burglars, etc, are desired immediately to bring or send the best description they can of such robbers, etc, with the time

and place and circumstances of the fact, to Henry Fielding Esq., at his house in Bow Street.

Nor did Fielding merely sit waiting for information, as another report from the *Gentleman's Magazine* of 6 March 1753 clearly shows:

> About four o'clock this morning, Justice Fielding having intelligence that some highwaymen were to be at a masquerade, went into the gaming room, with the officers on guard, and obliged all the company to unmask and give an account of themselves. It is supposed those fellows had notice of his coming before he could get up the stairs and so made off in the crowd, for none of them were taken.

Despite all Fielding's endeavours, however, crime in the city continued unabated, and hardly a day passed without an audacious robbery being committed, such as the one reported by the ever-alert Horace Walpole who wrote:

> I was sitting in my own dining-room on Sunday night, the clock had not struck eleven, when I heard a loud cry of 'Stop thief!' A highwayman had attacked a post-chaise in Piccadilly, within fifty yards of this house; the fellow was pursued, rode over the watchman, almost killed him, and escaped.

Fielding now put forward to the government an even more radical proposal: he wanted money to set up an organization of detectives. At first glance the idea seemed no more than a variation on the thief-taker, and, as there was still an aura of suspicion surrounding the very name, it might have seemed an idea without much chance of success. But what he had in mind was to keep the Bow Street office open day and night, with a magistrate always in attendance, plus two officers with horses, available to set off to the scene of any crime as soon as it was reported. These men were to be paid whether or not they ensured a conviction, and a fund was also to be established for buying information from informants and rewarding other helpful parties. Finally, Henry Fielding wanted a register compiled of all crimes and all suspected criminals, and the maximum publicity given to the activities of his 'runners' in the hope of deterring crime.

According to Fielding, the cost of setting up this force – to all intents and purposes the forerunner of the modern CID – would be an estimated £600 per year, and the result:

> the demolition of the reigning gangs, and the civil police put into such order that no such gangs should ever be able for the future to form themselves into bodies, or at least to remain for any time formidable.

These were bold words, and though Henry Fielding received a sympathetic hearing, the government took its time in making a decision – and then only allocated £400 per year. But something was better than nothing, and the two brothers plunged on with their work, breaking up several gangs and arresting a number of notorious highwaymen in the succeeding months.

However, the strain of all this work took its toll on Henry Fielding – he often worked as much as sixteen hours a day – and in 1754 his health had declined so much that John was forced to take over many of his tasks. In May of that year he retired, and shortly thereafter set off on a recuperative voyage to Lisbon, but was dead by October. Sadly, what posthumous fame has been accorded to the name of Henry Fielding is as the creator of *Tom Jones*, and it has taken the passage of time and the full development of the police-force for scholars to reassess his vital role in its creation.

John Fielding, who was then thirty-three, carried on the good work his brother had begun. 'Mr Fielding's People' now became a permanent force under the more familiar name of the Bow Street Runners; their motto 'quick notice and sudden pursuit'. John also commenced a determined campaign against the highwaymen which, in time, was to lead to the formation of the horse patrol and sound the death knell of the men of the roads.

Although the Fieldings are generally linked together in any discussion of their contributions to the history of crime, and John always insisted that he was merely carrying out Henry's ideas, that insistence was far too modest. For among the other achievements during his term of office was the creation of the Bow Street foot patrol; the founding of the *Hue and Cry*, a weekly journal full of court proceedings, reports of crimes and descriptions of wanted men, which later became the famous *Police Gazette*; and a pamphlet, *A Plan For Preventing Robberies within Twenty Miles of London*, which was specifically directed towards exterminating the highwaymen.

John's ahievements are all the more commendable when his blindness is remembered, for as Christopher Hibbert, in *The Roots of Evil* (1963), put it:

> He overcame his handicap without apparent difficulty, and was the first man to propose better street lighting to reduce crime. 'The Blind Beak', as he was called with affection, carried a small switch which he flicked in front of him as he walked briskly in and out of court ... A magistrate of rare integrity and great energy and intelligence, he directed his small force with extraordinary success.

One of John Fielding's first successes in office was the capture in 1754 of a villainous highwayman named Charles Fleming who had been a menace to travellers going from London to the north during the previous four years. The magistrate knew only too well, though, that there were still far too many highway robbers on the loose. He began trying to rouse public support by inserting notices such as this one which appeared in the *Public Advertiser* of October 1754:

> Whereas many thieves and robbers daily escape justice for want of immediate pursuit, it is therefore recommended to all persons who shall henceforth be robbed on the highway or in the streets, that they should give immediate notice therefore, together with as accurate a description as possible to John Fielding Esq at his house in Bow Street, Covent Garden; by which means, joined to an advertisement containing an account of the things lost, thieves and robbers will seldom escape, as most pawnbrokers take in this paper and by the intelligence they get from it assist daily in discovering and apprehending rogues.

John sensed that it was a mixture of fear and apathy which was enabling the highwaymen to continue their robberies, and he cited a case where a single masked man had attacked two men, one of them a Guards captain, in a post-chaise, on Hounslow Heath at two o'clock in the afternoon. But when the captain had released one of his horses and set off in pursuit of the robber, said the magistrate:

> it seemed incredible that notwithstanding the gentleman was not twenty yards behind him in the town of Hounslow and kept crying out, 'Highwayman! Highwayman!' as he pursued him, yet no one had spirit enough to join the pursuit.

It was enough to make anyone think the inhabitants of Hounslow actually wanted the highwayman to escape, John Fielding declared, and promptly began work on his *Plan for Preventing Robberies*. In this he proposed that twenty country gentlemen, living within twenty miles of London, should be recruited to send word to Bow Street as soon as they heard of any highway robbery. This would enable his runners to mount a pursuit and his office to send messages to turnpike-keepers, publicans and stable-keepers to keep watch for a wanted highwayman who might soon pass their way.

It was a plan that depended on good citizenship for success, and there were those sceptics who doubted it would ever succeed. Fielding, however, found enough gentlemen to co-operate, and was at once rewarded with success when a highwayman was arrested in London less than forty-eight hours after he had robbed a coach in Essex. Although it took him a while to convince the government of the effectiveness of his plan, he at last obtained another £200 towards his annual costs.

A glance at Fielding's records of expenditure at this time provides some interesting facts about the amounts being paid to those who co-operated with the runners. By far the largest sums were going to the informants on highwaymen: 'Waylaying a highwayman at a turnpike' earned one man five shillings; while the chap who 'Pursued a highwayman near Hackney' got seventeen shillings and six pence. Best of all – and doubtless rightly so – was the recipient of £8. 8s. for 'Pursuing and apprehending Jonathan Wigmore, highwayman, for attempting to rob the King of Poland's groom!'

In 1761, the 'Blind Beak' was knighted, marking this public recognition of his achievements by proposing the Bow Street horse patrol, a mounted and well-armed force who would be based near turnpikes to intercept or pursue highwaymen. For the first time, the forces of law would meet the forces of highway robbery on equal terms.

Fielding was given government approval and appointed ten officers whose nightly patrols began in the autumn of 1763. They were an immediate success – so successful, in fact, that when a sharp decline in the number of highway robberies was reported by Fielding to his masters, they firmly believed that an end had been put to the nation's highwaymen! However, when Fielding suggested the horse patrol should be made permanent to ensure freedom of travel, the government disagreed. There were to be no more funds.

It was a short-sighted decision, and even blind Sir John could see the inevitable outcome. As soon as his patrols disappeared from the roads, the highwaymen returned once more with renewed energy. A second attempt to revive the patrol was also short-lived and by 1770 it had been abandoned permanently. Although he had no way of knowing it at the time, Fielding had planted the seed that would later become the mounted police.

Sir John and his brother Henry had also set in motion the forces that would finally clear the roads of highwaymen. But that was still a little way off when John Fielding died in 1780, and it is sad to record that the importance of the Fieldings' achievements was a long time in being appreciated. For they had begun the process that would transform the thief-taker of the old world into the policeman of the new.

Bow Street remained London's police headquarters after Sir John's death, but it was not until 1805 that one of his successors, Sir Richard Ford, re-established the horse patrol, with a task-force of fifty-two men and a grant of £8,000 a year. Then, in 1822, Sir Robert Peel set up the first day-patrol of uniformed policemen, and seven years later introduced the Metropolitan Police Act which brought all the various forces under one administration and laid down proper regulations and conditions of service.

The dream of the Fielding brothers had at last become a reality, although neither man was around to see it. Nor, indeed, were those who had primarily brought about its inception: the highwaymen. For the last, some would say unique, members of their fraternity had also lived out their final chapter during those momentous years …

12 The Last Gallop into Legend

The English highwayman did not disappear in a final show of bravado as some other criminal groups in history have done. The best of them may well have been strongly individual characters, bold and romantic, with a sense of humour and an ability to face death with equanimity, but there was to be no last-ditch stand against the society they had challenged and so often mocked. Indeed, it was rather more a case of their numbers declining as the arm of the law became stronger and gradually extended from the environs of London out into the towns and countryside. Once, they had been safe just a few miles from the metropolis, but, as the second half of the seventeenth century drew on, the net grew ever tighter no matter how far they rode.

The Fielding brothers had been the catalysts for the decline of these years: first putting paid to the gangs of highway robbers, who were obviously easier to trace and arrest; then turning to the lone riders whose devil-may-care attitude and love of public attention too often proved their undoing. These last 'knights of the road' were, though, to prove worthy descendants of their forebears; dashing in the saddle and brave when the noose of Tyburn was placed around their necks. To a man, they were game to the very end.

An unusual departure from past practice was the number of these robbers who chose to work in pairs, both for mutual protection and effectiveness; whilst those who rode alone were just the kind of strikingly unique individuals to ensure the legend of the highwaymen would long survive their passing. Jack Rann, who roamed the highways in the 1770s in an unusual outfit that earned him the nickname 'Sixteen String Jack', was just such a character – and what makes his story even more interesting is that he was brought to justice by the dogged persistence of one of Sir John Fielding's best Bow Street Runners, John Clarke.

Jack Rann was born a few miles from Bath, in 1750. His parents were apparently tinkers and the child lead a wandering life until the age of twelve, when his curly brown hair and handsome face attracted the attention of a 'lady of fashion' who offered him a job in her service. This work took Jack to London, but did not hold him long and, by the age of twenty, he had variously been a stable-lad, postilion and coachman: all jobs which developed his knowledge of horses. It was while he was working in the last of these jobs for the Earl of Sandwich that he earned his famous nickname.

Jack had begun to show a love of fine clothes and ostentation soon after arriving in London, and he devised a novel way of distinguishing himself from the others in his position, as a late eighteenth-century newspaper report has explained:

> The breeches of grooms and postboys were laced at the knee, there being eight eyelet holes on each side of the openings, and the usual method was for one string or 'lace' to be used, passing to and fro across the opening to be tied at the knee in a workmanlike knot. This serviceable method would not do for Jack Rann. Instead, he had sixteen separate ribbons, each holding two of the eyelet holes together and each tied in a dainty bow. The peculiarity was so marked – perhaps so much admired – that to his delight he became known far and wide as 'Sixteen String Jack'.

Another legend has it that Jack earned his nickname by being arrested, charged and acquitted sixteen times for highway robbery, but there is no evidence to substantiate he was taken into custody on more than half this number of occasions.

Jack's fondness for finery was such that when he was not working he loved to dress in silk coats and flowered-satin waistcoats, but these things cost more money than a coachman could afford and he was soon in debt. He acquired the money by picking pockets with several other young men, including one lad named William Collier who came to admire his style so much that he copied his fashion and became known as 'Eight String Jack'.

In 1770, however, Jack was arrested in the act of picking a gentleman's pocket and put in Newgate to await trial. There he had his first glimpse of a highwayman and, seeing the way the fellow flung his money around and attracted women, vowed to ride in his footsteps. And, no sooner had he been fortuitously acquitted for lack of evidence on the stealing charge, than he secured a horse and some pistols and took to the road.

Vain 'Sixteen String Jack' may well have been, but he was no fool. For when he carried out his robberies he chose to wear what were described as 'the very meanest clothes', switching only into his fashionable suits and accoutrements when visiting a restaurant or gaming club. He also had an adoring mistress, a whore named Eleanor Roche, who he used to fence the proceeds of his robberies.

According to contemporary evidence, Jack Rann was arrested and charged with highway robbery on several occasions, though lack of evidence seems to have prevented him being successfully prosecuted. Then, on 30 May, 1772, Jack came face to face with the redoubtable Sir John Fielding. He was accused of holding up the coach of a Mr John Devall on Hounslow Road and robbing him of his watch and some money.

Although Jack was brought into court in leg-irons, he had on one of his smartest suits and carried 'a nosegay as big as a birch-broom'. In the dock he protested his innocence defiantly, while alongside him stood an equally stylishly dressed Eleanor Roche, charged with receiving.

Even under cross-examination from the 'Blind Beak', Jack carried his lying off bravely, even a little insolently. 'I know no more of the matter than you do,' he is said to have replied to Sir John; adding impudently, 'nor half so much, neither.'

This case, too, broke down because although Devall identified the watch, he could not swear that the dandy in the dock was the scruffy-looking man who had accosted him. Sir John had no alternative but to free Rann, although he called his officer John Clarke to one side and urged him to keep up his investigations into 'Sixteen String Jack'. Jack and Eleanor, for their part, left the court arm in arm for a celebratory meal in Vauxhall.

Less than two months later, Jack was back again before Sir John, charged this time with attempted house-breaking. However, he had merely been caught climbing through a window of his mistress's house in Covent Garden, as she had fallen asleep while waiting for him to return – in all probability from a highway robbery. But the fairminded magistrate had no alternative but to dismiss this case as well, though he did tell the smirking Jack, as he stood in the box, 'Your profession is perfectly well known, and I urge you to leave your evil courses while yet there is time.'

Jack, however, heeded not a word of this warning, continuing his highway robberies by day, and by night living 'a life of braggadocio and bombast that would be incredible if it were not proved beyond shadow of doubt', according to a contemporary report. All the time, though, the resolute John Clarke continued to tail his man, hoping to secure the evidence that would finally bring an end to 'Sixteen String Jack's' career.

An event which helped ensure Jack's notoriety occurred about this time when he turned up at Tyburn for an execution dressed in an outrageous scarlet coat, tambour waistcoat and silk stockings. A ring of constables were keeping the crowd back, but Jack is said to have bribed one to let him through the barrier and stand close to the prisoner's cart.

'It is very proper I should be a spectator on this occasion,' he is said to have boasted, 'since I, myself, am a celebrated highwayman!'

Needless to say the man being hanged was a highway robber, and this was surely Jack's way of having a dig at the alleged deterrent value of capital punishment!

Jack is also remembered for another scene, at the fashionable resort of Bagnigge Wells, when he suddenly announced to a group of admirers that he appeared to have lost a valuable ring from his finger. Had it been stolen, he wondered. Then, ' 'Tis no matter,' he is reported to have said; ' 'tis but a hundred guineas gone, and one evening's work will replace it.'

But no man could expect to boast so openly of his crimes and avoid retribution when a custodian of the law such as Sir John Fielding had his measure. And on 26 September, 1774 Jack, with his faithful neophyte, 'Eight String Jack', committed the robbery that brought him to the gallows. A newspaper report states:

> In company they robbed Dr. William Bell, chaplain to the Princess Amelia on the Uxbridge road. As the reverend doctor was riding near Ealing he was overtaken by two men of suspicious appearance, one of whom suddenly rode across his

front and demanded his money with the usual threats. Dr. Bell gave all he had: eighteen pence and a common watch in a tortoiseshell case. Watches were fatal to Rann and this second time-keeper led to his arrest.

It was the persistent John Clarke who assembled the evidence for the subsequent hearing before his chief. Meanwhile, Jack waited in Newgate, confident as ever of acquittal and even making plans for a celebratory supper. But this time there was to be no disputing the good Dr Bell's evidence, and he added considerable weight to his statement by declaring that he knew the prisoner well by sight, having seen him parading about London.

Sir John had no difficulty pronouncing his verdicts: Rann was to go to the gallows; William Collier was also found guilty, but recommended for mercy; while Eleanor Roche was sentenced to fourteen years transportation. For Jack the end had come, but 'Eight String Jack' was later reprieved and was never heard of again.

The bravado that was so much a part of Jack Rann's character did not desert him: on Sunday 27 November three days before his execution, he went ahead with his planned party in his cell, seven whores being among his guests, and he 'in the gayest good spirits, declaring, "let us eat, drink and be merry, for tomorrow we die." '

This account of his last days continues:

> He was still the life and soul of the party, and the gay smile was still on his face, when he was driven to Tyburn, resplendent in yet another brand new pea-green suit and ruffled shirt. At the gallows the huge crowd gazed admiringly as the cart drove off and his incomparable buckskin breeches dangled into view and the usual convulsive movements of his legs fluttered the famous sixteen silk strings about his knees.

Is it any wonder that the great Dr Johnson was so impressed by this man that he should draw a parallel, when writing later of the poetry of Thomas Gray, that he thought it towered above that of the ordinary poet 'as Sixteen String Jack towered above the common highwayman'?

John Clarke, who had seen Rann brought to justice, was also responsible for tracking down two famous highwaymen brothers, George and Joseph Weston, who are unique in highway history as there is no other case on record of two highway robbers coming from a single family.

George Weston was born in 1753, and his younger brother Joseph in 1759, the sons of a Staffordshire farmer. In 1772, the elder boy was sent to London to work for a merchant, but soon began to live a dissipated life beyond his means. When Joseph followed him and fell into the same life of gambling and whoring, the pair quickly ran up debts and had to make a hasty departure when creditors came looking for their money.

The two brothers thereafter lived a colourful life including touring as actors with a party of strolling players (no doubt good training for the displays of bravado every highwayman needed to show), horse-trading, farming, and selling dubious foreign goods, before gradually sliding into confidence tricks, forgery and smuggling. Often the pair posed as master and man; sometimes as a squire and his servant; at other times a rich young dandy and his companion. All in all they lived in some comfort, though constantly on the move about the country to avoid the law.

It was when the pair were travelling from Bristol to Bath on 29 January 1781 and overtook a Royal Mail coach, that George decided they had found their true vocation. Not for him any ordinary traveller with a few gold coins in his pocket, rather a GPO carriage packed with bank-notes and bills! Handing Joseph a piece of black cloth from his pocket and putting another piece around his own fence, George took out a pistol and proceeded to halt the mail-cart. Having bound the driver, they seized the cart, complete with its baggage, and rode off.

A report prepared by the mail office was in circulation within hours of the discovery of the robbery and appeared in the newspapers the following morning. A copy has survived and reads, in part:

> The postboy bringing the Bristol Mail this morning from Maidenhead was stopped between two and three o'clock by a single Highwayman with a crepe over his face between the 11th and 12th milestones, near to Cranford Bridge, who presented a pistol to him, and after making him alight drove away the Horse and Cart which were found about 7 o'clock this morning in a meadow field near Farmer Lott's at Twyford, when it appears

> that the greatest part of the letters were taken out of the Bath and Bristol bags.
>
> The person who committed this robbery is supposed to have had an accomplice, as two persons passed the Postboy on Cranford Bridge on Horseback prior to the Robbery, one of whom he thinks was the robber; but it being so extremely dark, he is not able to give any description of their persons.

The report added that a reward of £200 was being posted for the apprehension and conviction of the highwaymen.

When the Westons counted out their loot they could hardly believe their eyes: the value of the bank-notes and bills was approximately £15,000 – probably the largest haul of any highway robbery! But, realizing that a description of these notes would soon be circulated, George put another plan into operation. The brothers returned to London, hired themselves a post-chaise and thereafter set off on a 'grand tour' of the country. Over the next few weeks they visited town after town exchanging the notes and bills to pay for their accommodation and purchases, accepting only coins in return.

By December 1781, the Westons had dispersed enough of their booty to begin new lives under assumed names. Posing as two gentlemen of means, Mr William Johnson and Mr Samuel Watson, they leased a large house in Winchelsea and were soon accepted members of the local society. To complete this front of respectability, the pair also procured 'wives': a couple of women, two cousins who had previously been employed as milliners, to share their extravagant lifestyle.

Unbeknownst to the Westons, however, the Royal Mail office had called in the Bow Street Runners to help in their investigations, and the experienced John Clarke was now on the case. First he found the coachman who had driven the two gentlemen on their 'grand tour'; he then methodically began to follow the trail of encashed bills. Before he left London, though, Clarke posted descriptions of his suspects which showed just how thorough his investigations were proving:

> George Weston is about 29 years of age, 5 ft 7 inches high, square set, round faced, fresh coloured, pitted with smallpox, has a rather thick nose, his hair of lightest brown colour, which is sometimes tied behind, and at other times loose and curled; has much the appearance of a country dealer or farmer. One of his

> thumb nails appears, from an accident, of the shape of a parrot's bill.
>
> Joseph Weston is about 23 years of age, 5 ft 9 inches high, slender made, of fair and smooth complexion, genteel person, has grey eyes and large nose with a scar upon it; his hair is of a light brown colour, sometimes tied behind, at other times loose and curled; his voice is strong and he speaks a little through his nose; has a remarkable small hand and long fingers.

In Winchelsea, Messrs 'Johnson' and 'Watson' enjoyed the lives of respectable if somewhat extravagant local citizens, until some unpaid bills brought creditors to their door and they were forced to look for a new hiding-place once again. They opted for London – and there Sir John Fielding's scheme for paying informers paid off, when John Clarke received word that the two men described in his advertisement were staying at a hotel in Wardour Street. It was the deformed thumbnail of one of the men that had given him away.

When Clarke arrived, the two tried to make a run for it, but after a brief exchange of pistol fire, they were overpowered – thanks to some public-spirited citizens who, their consciences perhaps pricked by Sir John's earlier remarks, joined in the arrest. On both men were found the last of the bank-notes they had stolen from the Bristol Mail.

During their preliminary hearing, the Weston brothers kept up a show of bravado, George actually shouting at John Clarke that he was 'fortunate in still having his brains in his skull'. Their show of arrogance had much to do with the fact that the most crucial witness against them, the post boy, Samuel Walker, had died in the interim. They were still, however, committed for trial on 2 July 1782.

While the pair were imprisoned at Newgate, they lived in the same manner as Jack Rann, entertaining lavishly, and planning with their two 'wives' a daring prison break. The girls slipped their consorts files with which they proceeded to remove their fetters; then, overpowering a guard, they made a run for cover. George and Joseph were no Jack Sheppards, however, and although they separated, both were in custody again by nightfall thanks to the efficiency of Judge Fielding's Bow Street Runners.

The trial of the two highwaymen for robbing the mail began on 6 July and over one hundred witnesses – many of them people who had been paid with the stolen notes – produced an overwhelming case against them. The Westons were found guilty and hanged together at Tyburn on 3 September a report in the *Annual Register* of the time describing them as 'two most notorious villains, who for some years have defrauded the country by various artful contrivances'.

This was not the end of their story, however, for their exploits caught the interest of the writer George Makepeace Thackeray, who featured them in his half-finished novel, *Dennis Duval.* However, unlike most other works, which romanticized highway robbers, Thackeray's book painted the brothers as a pair of villains and was intended to 'counteract the injurious influence of some fiction of the day which makes heroes of highwaymen'.

What Thackeray could not do, however, was prevent them earning a unique mention in highway history which time has done nothing to erase.

The last decade of the century also saw another pair of highwaymen achieve widespread notoriety – their names were Jerry Abershaw and Richard 'Galloping Dick' Ferguson. Abershaw has remained the more famous of the partnership, primarily because a number of historians have persisted in calling him 'The Last of the Highwaymen' which, as I shall show, he most certainly was not.

The enduring fame of this pair owes much to their entries in the *Newgate Calendar* and to George Borrow who refers to them, in *Romany Rye*, as 'two most awful fellows who enjoyed a long career'. And, discussing their respective merits he adds, 'capital rider as Abershaw certainly was, he was decidedly inferior to Richard Ferguson, generally called "Galloping Dick".'

As the two men did not meet until Abershaw was already a well-known highwayman, it is necessary to look at their earlier life stories separately, beginning with Jerry Abershaw, who R.L. Hadfield has described in his book, *Picturesque Rogues* (1951), as 'the last of the genuine highwaymen'. He then paints this glowing word-picture of the man:

> Here was no sneak-thief, robbing old women or unarmed men and scurrying into hiding at the slightest sign of danger; here was no common assassin who would shoot a defenceless man down just to shut his mouth, as the highly overrated Turpin did. Jerry had something of the swaggering carelessness of the consequences about him that has given glamour to the calling of highwaymen. He was a brave man and, though a robber who

> deserved his fate, seems to have succeeded, if one can use such a term in this connection, in 'playing the game'.

Jerry was born in Kingston upon Thames, in 1773. His real name was actually Louis Jeremiah Avershaw and his parents were 'poor but honest folk', to quote the same biographer. The boy took to horses as a child and obtained his first job as the driver of a post-chaise when still in his early teens. Quite what turned him into a highway robber, however, has never been established (other than an obvious love of adventure), but his first hold-ups were committed in a nearby spot known as Putney Bottom, through which the Portsmouth road ran on its way to Kingston.

By the age of seventeen, Jerry was the leader of an occasional band of highwaymen who used a public house, the Bald Faced Stag at Beverley Brook, as a meeting point. When he worked on his own, Jerry's favourite haunts were Putney Heath and Wimbledon Common, and he appears to have enjoyed five successful and untroubled years in these locations. Among the explanations that have been offered for his success at this time when the Bow Street Runners were becoming ever more vigilant was the fact that he did not boast of his exploits like so many of his kind and had no regular female companion who might betray his movements. It was to be a woman he met occasionally for sex, however, who would bring about his fateful meeting with Richard Ferguson ...

Ferguson was born in 1775, the son of a land steward, who had him well educated and then placed in work as a stable-boy. Richard, however, was a rather headstrong lad with a keen interest in the opposite sex, and, when an affair with one of his employer's maids was discovered, he was dismissed. He was thereafter in and out of work until his father died in 1790 and left him an inheritance of fifty-seven pounds. Not much today, but certainly a windfall in those days. Richard promptly took himself off to London where he hoped to live the life of a young gentleman.

His head, though, was soon turned by a pretty whore he met in Drury Lane, and though he knew she had a number of other admirers, including a highwayman, he continued to pursue her until his money ran out. Then, on his way to his last night of extravagance with the girl, he saw another man just leaving her house. Although he had no way of knowing it, the man was Jerry Abershaw – who was in the habit of making occasional visits to the city for a little female company.

By now penniless, Richard had to seek work as a postilion; and fate provided him with a second meeting with Jerry Abershaw, when the highwayman held up a coach he was driving along the Great North Road. A gust of wind chanced to lift up the assailant's mask and in the moonlight his face was clearly visible to the young man. As the highwayman rode away from the scene he, too, realized that he had seen Ferguson before, and where they had met.

As he rode, Abershaw decided it was imperative to double back and follow the coach to its next stop to buy the postilion's silence. When he confronted the young man at an inn, however, he was told he could do better than that – he could teach him to be a highwayman, because there was obviously a lot more money to be made from it than in his present occupation!

Impressed by Richard Ferguson's spirit and nerve, Jerry agreed and the young man soon proved a good accomplice and, in time, an excellent associate. Ferguson also followed the older man's lead by operating sometimes on his own and sometimes with others. It was, in fact, when he was out with two other highwaymen on the Edgware Road and they ill-advisedly picked on a party of travellers who proved to be well armed, that he earned his nickname.

Such was the speed of the pursuers that only Richard was able to escape: the other two men were caught, brought to trial, and hanged. Complimented on this feat by some admiring friends, Ferguson boasted he could 'gallop a horse with any man in the Kingdom' – and was thereafter known as 'Galloping Dick'.

Abershaw and Ferguson proved a formidable partnership whenever they rode out together, but Jerry met his moment of fate on his own. He was in a Southwark public house when he was suddenly cornered by two Bow Street Runners, David Price and Bernard Turner, who had been on his trail after being 'sold' information on his whereabouts. Although Abershaw made a desperate attempt to escape, by firing at the two men as they entered the inn – mortally wounding Price and seriously injuring Turner – he was nonetheless arrested. Turner, happily, made a good recovery and was able to provide the damming evidence at the highwayman's trial at the Croydon assizes on 30 July 1795.

Jerry remained unperturbed throughout the case. When the judge, Mr Baron Pentryn, put on the black cap to pronounce sentence, he mimicked him by putting on his own hat. And later in his prison cell he ordered black cherries and for the first time spoke about his career – using the juice of the berries to draw pictures of his exploits on the walls!

Abershaw was hanged not at Tyburn but on Kennington Common – the gallows standing on a piece of land today occupied by football pitches – and the report in the *Public Advertiser* describes a moment of grim humour the prisoner introduced into the event:

> On the way to execution, he kept up an incessant conversation with the persons who rode beside the cart, frequently laughing and nodding to others of his acquaintance whom he perceived in the crowd, which was immense. Arrived there, he kicked off his boots among the crowd and died unshod, to disprove an old saying of his mother's, that he was a bad lad, and would die in his shoes.

According to another contemporary source, the highwayman's body was afterwards hung in chains in his old haunt of Putney Bottom:

> and an old and nasty legend was long current in those parts of a sergeant in a regiment soon afterwards marching past firing at the distended body, by which (to make short of an offensive story) the neighbourhood was nearly poisoned. The sergeant was reduced to the ranks for this ill-judged choice of a target.

Abershaw was just twenty-two when he was hanged, and though Richard Ferguson was undoubtedly sad at having lost his partner-in-crime, he nevertheless continued to operate on the same highways for another five years, the fleetness of his horse more than once enabling him to escape the Bow Street Runners, who were now tracking him as resolutely as they had done his mentor.

Although there are no specific details of Ferguson's later crimes, Charles Harper provides this intriguing summary of the rest of his career:

> The name of 'Galloping Dick' became well known and was a name of dread. No clattering horseman could come hurriedly along the road without stirring the pulses of nervous travellers,

who immediately fancied 'Galloping Dick' was upon them. Indeed, he soon became too well known for any degree of safety, and he would then for a while, for prudential reasons, find temporary employment as a postilion.

He was at last arrested by the Bow Street Runners at the beginning of 1800 and charged at Aylesbury for having committed a highway robbery in Buckinghamshire. He was sent for trial to the Lent Assizes, convicted, and soon after executed.

The death of Richard Ferguson did not pass without being commemorated in a typical halfpenny broadsheet – though this one may well have been read with a great sense of relief by all those travellers who had for years feared hearing the sound of his horse galloping up behind them:

> Galloping Dick took a hasty road to perdition. Happy had it been for him had he chosen the safe path of virtue, and run a good race.

Despite the fact that a new century had now dawned, the race of the highwaymen themselves was not yet quite run. There is, however, some disagreement amongst historians as to whether the men of the road survived into the nineteenth century. Charles Harper, for instance, argues 'It was still, at the close of the eighteenth century, abundantly possible for peaceful travellers along the roads to be killed by highwaymen;' while Patrick Pringle states, 'The Age of the Highwaymen only just intrudes on the nineteenth century.'

And so often in such cases, the truth lies somewhere between these two points of view.

The very last year of the old century saw a Mr Mellish wantonly killed by an unknown highwayman at Sipson Green on the Bath road. Mr Mellish, who was a city merchant, was returning with two friends in his coach after a day's hunting, when the party was held up. All three men handed over their money and valuables without protest and the carriage was actually on the move again towards Bath when a shot rang out from the highwayman's pistol and struck Mr Mellish in the forehead. He died before medical attention could be found for him. What is puzzling about this case is whether the robber intended to hit the merchant – which seems unlikely as he already had his spoils – or was merely warning the coach passengers that he would shoot if any attempt was made to retaliate.

Whichever is the case, the highwayman was never brought to justice. But there were others, like John Haines, who suffered the fate of gibbeting on Hounslow Heath in May 1799. This particular execution merited a few lines in the *Annual Register*, offering proof – if any is needed – that the spectacle of highwaymen being put to death was a popular sight.

The *Register* relates how a party of eight gentlemen who had been to watch John Haines 'turned off', ferried over the Thames to the Flower Pot Inn at Sunbury at about ten o'clock in the evening, presumably intent on carrying on the drinking they had enjoyed during the day. However, it was an ill-advised plan, for during the crossing the boat was upset and three of the men were drowned.

The omens for highwaymen in the new century were certainly not good, either. Following the passing, in 1797, of Pitt's Act for Restricting Cash Payments, there were now fewer people travelling the roads with large sums of money on their persons; while banking and the payment of money by cheque had grown considerably among the gentry. Whereas previously men and women had travelled the countryside with often surprisingly large sums of money, they now took bank-notes and only those valuables that were easily identifiable: both being types of property that the Fielding brothers had now made it difficult to handle unlawfully.

By combing the records, however, it is still possible to find further evidence of highwaymen after the time of Jerry Abershaw. In April 1802, for instance, William Whalley was hanged at Horsham in front of a crowd of 3,000 for robbing the Royal Mail at East Grinstead of £1,700 in bank-notes and valuables worth £1,000. A few months later one Richard Smith was executed at Finchley for robbing several coachmen on the highways out of London.

There is rather more evidence about Robert Snooks who saw a chance for riches by robbing the mail. Born in Hungerford, Snooks was first heard of operating as a highwayman in the area of Hemel Hempstead, Hertfordshire, in 1800. The following year he held up the mail-carrier on what was then a lonely stretch of land known as Boxmoor and made off with money and valuables worth in excess of £1,500. Believing that it might be safe to spend this booty in London, Snooks moved to Southwark; but it could hardly have been long before he saw the advertisements in the newspapers, offering £300 for his capture.

After one ill-fated attempt to pass a bank-note with the aid of a maid-servant, Snooks rode back to Hungerford and appears to have lived there unnoticed for the best part of a year until he was informed upon by a former school-friend. By a cruel twist of fate, this friend was now working as a post boy and happened to see Robert riding a horse while he was delivering. Snooks was duly tried at the Hertford assizes and sentenced to death.

This could well have been the end of the story of Robert Snooks had he not died in the best highwayman tradition: so he is remembered by a memorial stone which can still be viewed today.

The judge at Snook's trial decided to make an example of him by hanging him at the scene of his last crime, on Boxmoor – although a plan to leave his gibbeted body there, in chains, was overruled by the more sensitive souls on the jury. The highwayman, who was by all accounts a tall and rather handsome man, made the journey from Hertford gaol to Boxmoor in good spirits, stopping at the Swan Inn on Box Lane to take the obligatory last glass of ale and remarking to some spectators passing by, 'Don't hurry – there'll be no fun till I get there!'

On the gallows, Snooks gave a final address to the assembled crowds which was copied down and still survives. As the last existing 'confession' by a highwayman it is, I think, worth quoting here in full:

> Good people, I beg your particular attention to my fate. I hope this lesson will be of more service to you than the gratification of the curiosity which brought you here. I beg to caution you against evil doings, and most earnestly entreat you to avoid two evils, namely 'Disobedience to parents' – to you youths I particularly give this caution – and, 'The breaking of the Sabbath'. These misdeeds lead to the worst of crimes: robbery, plunder, bad women, and every evil course. It may by some be thought a happy state to be in possession of fine clothes and plenty of money, but I assure you no one can be happy with ill-gotten treasure. I have often been riding on my horse and passed a cottager's door, whom I have seen dressing his greens, and perhaps had hardly a morsal to eat with them. He has very likely envied me in my

> station, who, though at that time in possession of abundance, was miserable and unhappy. I envied him, and with most reason, for his happiness and contentment. I can assure you there is no happiness but in doing good. I justly suffer for my offences, and hope it will be a warning to others. I die in peace with God and all the world.

It was an eloquent speech, and there was hardly a sound from the crowd as the horse pulling the cart in which Snooks stood was whipped up and drew away from the gallows. The highwayman's courage had touched everyone, and there were those who were unhappy to see his corpse thrown into a shallow grave nearby. Indeed, the next day a party of them returned, dug up the body and reburied it in a coffin. Two pieces of pudding-stone were laid down to mark the spot.

Although a local tradition maintains that Snook's body was later dug up a second time by body-snatchers who made off with it, the site of the grave still exists on Boxmoor not far from a roadside inn called the Friend at Hand. About 150 yards away, on the opposite side of the road is a barren space of earth with a little mound and an inscribed stone. It was placed there in 1905 and reads simply: 'Robert Snooks, 11 March, 1802.'

There is nothing else to indicate that here lies one of the last English highwaymen. Not *the* last, but certainly the last to have died in the best tradition of his 'profession'.

As has already been mentioned, the establishment of the Bow Street patrol in 1805 did much to sweep the remaining highwaymen from the English roads – and certainly, by the time Robert Peel brought in his Metropolitan Police Bill in 1829, 'the highwayman had long been in his grave', according to Patrick Pringle.

In truth, there are only records of two more men of the road to demand our attention. One because his career was brought to an end in a bloody show-down; the other because he escaped into the night and thenceforth into the realms of legend.

George Allen was a Sussex man raised on a farm, who followed his instinct for excitement and adventure first into military service and then on to the roads of his native county. For the opening years of the nineteenth century, he made a profitable living on the highways between Arundel and Chichester, his special victims being farmers coming home from market after selling their livestock or produce.

Allen, who was always heavily disguised and mounted on a fast black horse, struck his victims swiftly and was gone into the night with their proceeds almost before they realized what had happened. However, such a menace did he become that the local farming community finally appealed to the military for help.

In the spring of 1807, a trap was set for Allen by the militia near the village of Midhurst, and, although he initially escaped their gunfire, his horse was wounded and he had not ridden far before the brave animal collapsed beneath him. At this, the highwayman turned to face his pursuers and died in a salvo of fire.

George Cutterman was the very last highwayman about whom records exist. He robbed on a notorious stretch of the Great North Road called Leeming Lane in north Yorkshire, which had been known for centuries as 'The Street'. When George's moment of fame came in 1812 he was known far and wide as 'The Highwaymen of Leeming Lane' – and so he has remained.

Leeming Lane was apparently 'a hot-bed of mounted and masked desperados', according to Cutterman's biographer, J. Fairfax-Blakeborough in *The Hand of Glory: Legends of Highwaymen and Others* (1924), who says that until the early years of the nineteenth century most sensible travellers made a point of traversing this section of road in convoys, for safety. Just when it seemed the efforts of the law-makers were at last cleaning up the road's reputation, a new highwayman began to rob travellers, in particular local cattle dealers. Fairfax-Blakeborough continues:

> Success seemed to embolden this mystery man as his impudent thefts continued, despite all the attempts made to earn the reward for his capture. He was like a will-o'-the-wisp – now here, now there, now mounted, now on foot, always relentless, and entirely devoid of either the courtesy or generosity of the general run of highwaymen, who only aimed at big game and often took toll from the rich to give to the poor. Among other robberies this mystery man – for not even a nick-name could yet be given to him – successfully carried out was the theft of an inheritance of £200 from an elderly couple who lived near Catterick.

Efforts were redoubled to try and capture the robber – including the posting of a reward of 100 guineas – but as so few facts were known about him, there was little optimism. Indeed, the man seemed to be laughing at his pursuers when he held up one of the most important coaches running between London and Edinburgh, 'The Highflyer'. The reward money was promptly increased to 200 guineas.

Because of the ease with which the mystery man seemed to disappear after each robbery, it began to be suggested that he might live in the vicinity: indeed, he could even be someone known in the area. Then, after the robbery of a butcher near the King's Head inn at Kirklington, the net began to tighten. For, during the course of enquiries, it was discovered that the landlord of the King's Head, George Cutterman, had been missing during the hour or so of the robbery; and in fact had not been around when the earlier hold-ups had taken place, either.

Officers of the law were therefore summoned from York to take the landlord into custody for questioning. Fairfax-Blakeborough concludes his account, which, he says, is based on evidence collected at the time by his father:

> When the lawmen arrived, Cutterman, with a fearful oath, made a furious dash for liberty; but almost as if by machinery he was tripped up and handcuffed before he knew what had happened. Ten minutes search put beyond all doubt Cutterman's guilt. Almost the first convicting proof which they discovered was the bundle of notes belonging to the old couple near Catterick. Then in a secret drawer in Cutterman's bureau was found the mask worn on his expeditions, and other property recognised as having been stolen.

The news of the arrest of the local landlord as a highwayman soon spread through Kirklington, and there were many shouts of abuse as the handcuffed figure was bundled into a coach for the ride to York. A voice was heard to call out from the crowd as the carriage pulled away that the same fate which had awaited other highway robbers like Dick Turpin was now in store for George Cutterman. The facts, however, proved otherwise. Fairfax-Blakeborough adds:

> But Cutterman was not hanged, nor did he ever reach York. When on top of the coach he persuaded his gaolers to remove his handcuffs, and as they considered him quite safe between them there, they acquiesced. Cutterman waited his opportunity, and as the coach was passing a load of hay he took a flying leap, and sliding down from the wagon, sped away with the fleetness of one

who knew that his life was at stake. A hue and cry was raised, but Cutterman was never either heard of or seen again.

With the disappearance of George Cutterman the era of the highwaymen came, finally, to an end. No more would these strikingly dressed figures on horseback, their features hidden by masks and with pistols held in each hand, ride out upon unwary travellers. Their time had come and gone: law, science and society had brought about their end. All that remained was their legend, a colourful slice of English history that is still just as fascinating today as it has been at any time during the intervening two hundred years. And doubtless, on the evidence of these pages, it will remain so for the foreseeable future.

Appendix: The Literature of the Highwaymen

During my research for this book I came across a number of fascinating pamphlets and broadsheets published at the time of the execution of several of the most notorious highwaymen. Although there was no space to include these items in the main text of the book, I felt they were worthy of a place and so they are reprinted here for the interest of the reader.

To the Memory of Captain Hind: By a Poet of His Own Time

(From a broadsheet published in September 1652)

Whenever Death attacks a throne,
Nature through all her parts must groan,
The mighty monarch to bemoan.

He must be wise, and just, and good,
Though not the state he understood,
Nor ever spared a subject's blood.

And shall no friendly poet find
A monumental verse for Hind? –
In fortune less, as great in mind.

Hind made our wealth one common store,
He robbed the rich to feed the poor;
What did immortal Caesar more?

Nay, 'twere not difficult to prove
That meaner views did Caesar move:
His was ambition, Hind's was love.

Our English Hero sought no crown,
Nor that more pleasant bait, renown;
But just to keep off Fortune's frown.

Yet when his country's cause invites,
See him assert a nation's rights!
A robber for his monarch fights.

If in due light his deeds we scan
As Nature points us out the plan,
Hind was an honourable man.

Honour, the virtue of the brave,
To Hind that turn of genius gave
Which made him scorn to be a slave.

Thus had his stars conspired to raise
His natal hour, this virtue's praise
Had shone with an uncommon blaze.

Some epoch had begun
From every action he had done –
A city built – a battle won.

If one's a subject, one at helm,
'Tis the same violence, says Anselm,
To rob a house or waste a realm.

Be henceforth, then, for ever joined
The names of Caesar and of Hind –
In fortunes different – one in mind.

Duval's Speech

(A copy of the 'dying confession' allegedly written in his own hand by Claude Duval, to be delivered at Tyburn on 21 January, 1670, and afterwards found in the pocket of his coat. It was published in a pamphlet issued a few days after the famous French highwayman's execution.)

> I should be very ungrateful (which, amongst persons of honour, is a greater crime than that for which I die) should I not acknowledge my obligation to you, fair English ladies. I could not have hoped that a person of my nation,

birth, education, and condition, would have had so many powerful charms to captivate you all, and to tie you so firmly to my interest that you have not abandoned me in distress, or in prison, that you have accompanied me to this place of death, of ignominious death. From the experience of your true loves I speak it; nay, I know I speak your hearts; you could be content to be with me now, and even here, could you be assured of enjoying your beloved Du Vall in the other world. How mightily, and how generously have you rewarded my little services. Shall I ever forget that universal consternation amongst you when I was taken, your frequent, your chargeable [costly] visits to me at Newgate, your shrieks, your swoonings when I was condemned, your zealous intercession and importunity for my pardon? You could not have erected fairer pillars of honour and respect to me, had I been an Hercules, and could have got fifty sons in a night. It has been the misfortune of several English gentlemen, in the times of the late usurpation, to die at this place upon the honourablest occasion that ever presented itself, the endeavouring to restore their exiled sovereign; gentlemen, indeed, who had ventured their lives, and lost their estates, in the service of their prince; but they all died unlamented and uninterceded for, because they were English. How much greater, therefore, is my obligation, whom you love better than your own countrymen, better than your own dear husbands? Nevertheless, ladies, it does not grieve me that your intercession for my life proved ineffectual; for now I shall die with little pain, an healthful body, and I hope a prepared mind. For my confessor has showed me the evil of my way, and wrought in me a true repentance; witness these tears, these unfeigned tears. Had you prevailed for my life, I must in gratitude have devoted it wholly to you, which yet would have been but short; for, had you been sound, I should soon have died of a consumption; if otherwise, of the Pox.

Dick Turpin's Confession

(This pamphlet was first published in the year of Turpin's execution, 1739, by Ward & Chandler of Temple Bar, London and Coney Street, York, and was sold for the considerable sum of sixpence per copy. It was, nonetheless, a huge seller and reprinted at least half a dozen times, although its authenticity is certainly very much open to question!)

The following account Turpin gave of himself to the Topsman the week after his Condemnation and repeated the same particulars to him again at the Gallows, which being taken down from his own Mouth, are as follows:

That he was bred a Butcher and served five years of his Time very faithfully in White-Chappel but falling into idle Company he began to make unlawful Measures to support his Extravagances and went some time on the Highway on Foot, and met with several small Booties, his not being detected therein gave him Encouragement to steal Horses and pursue his new Trade in Epping Forest on Horseback which he had continued about six years. Having been out one whole day without any Booty and being much tired, he laid himself down in the thicket and turned his Horse loose, having first taken off the saddle. When he wak'd, he went to search after his Horse and meeting with Mr Thompson's Servant he enquired if he had seen his Horse. To which Mr Thompson's man answered That he knew nothing of Turpin's Horse, but that he had found Turpin and accordingly presented his Blunderbuss at Turpin, who instantly Jumping behind a Broad Oak, avoided the Shot, and instantly fired a Carbine at Thompson's Servant and Shot him Dead on the Spot, one Slug went through his Breast, another through his Right Thigh, and a Third through his Groin. This done, he withdrew to a Yew Tree hard by, where he concealed himself so closely, that though the noise of Mr Thompson's Man's Blunderbuss and his own Carbine had drawn together a great Number of People about the Body, yet he continued undiscovered two whole Days and one Night in the tree, when the Company was all dispersed he got out of the Forest, and took a Black Horse out of a Close near the Road, and there being people working in the Field at a Distance he threw some Money amongst them, and made off, but afterwards the same Evening stole a Chestnut Mare and turning the Black Horse loose, made the best of his way for London, some Time after he returned to the Forest again and attempted to rob Captain Thompson and his Lady in an open Chaise but the Captain firing a Carbine at him, which missed and fired a Pistol after the Captain which went through the Chaise between him and his Lady without any further Damage, than tearing the Left Sleeve of his Coat, the Captain driving hard, and being Just in sight of a Town, Turpin thought it not proper to pursue him any further.

He next stopped a Country Gentleman whom he bade stop, but the gentleman clapped spurs to his horse and rode off, he rode after him, and fired a Pistol, which lodged two balls in his horse's buttocks so that gentleman was obliged to stop.

After this he stopped a Farmer in Epping Forest who had been to London to sell Hay, and took from him fifty shillings, and hearing of several Coaches coming that way, laid in wait for them but they being informed of the frequent robberies in those parts, took another road.

Another time meeting a Gentleman and Lady on Horseback in a Lane near the Forest he stopped them and presented a Pistol, at which the Lady fell into a Swoon, he took from the Gentleman seven Guineas and some Silver and from the Lady a Watch, A Diamond Ring, one Guinea and fifteen shillings in Silver.

He likewise owned that he was a Confederate with one King, who was executed in London some time since, and that, once being very near taken, he fired a Pistol amongst the Crowd, and by mistake, shot the said King in the Thigh who was coming to rescue him.

He also confessed the facts of which he was convicted, but said, many things had been laid to his charge of which he was innocent. Tho 'tis very probable he was guilty of several robberies not here mentioned, yet this was the whole confession that the Topsman could get from him.

The Female Robber: Or, Turpin's Sister

(This ballad, which was apparently a popular seller for a number of years around the middle of the eighteenth century, is another piece of evidence about highwaywomen. Although there is no suggestion that the heroine was an actual relative of Dick Turpin, the title is an indication of how familiar his name had become in the years following his execution.)

Ye females of every nation,
   Give ear to my frolicksome song,
The like was ne'er known in the nation,
   'Twas done by a female so young.

She bought her a horse and a bridle,
   With saddle and pistols also,
Resolving not to remain idle,
   But out on the highway she'd go.

She clothed herself with great splendour,
   Her breeches and sword she had on,
Her body appeared mighty slender,
   'Twas dressed like a pretty young man.

And thus like a robber so pretty,
   She mounted with speed on her mare,
She left all her friends in the city,
   And steered her course toward Ware.

The first she met was a grocer,
   Walking with a cane in his hand,
She soon to the spark rode up closer
   And boldly she bade him to stand.

She took from him only one guinea,
   The next was a tailor with shears,
Because the poor rogue had no money
   She nimbly cut off both his ears.

There was too a pinching old tanner,
   For the loss of his money he cried,
Because the poor rogue bawled so loudly
   She bravely tanned his hide.

The next was an honest exciseman,
She told him she must have the prise,
She robbed him of eighty gold guineas
Which he had received for excise.

The next was a cheating quack doctor
Whose clothes were all daubed o'er with lace,
She took both his clothes and his money,
It was a most pitiful case.

The next was an honest old lawyer,
At Assizes he pleaded the Laws,
She took both his watch and his money,
And this was the truth of the cause.

The next was a greasy fat landlord,
Whose paunch held a hogshead of beer,
She ransacked him of forty gold guineas,
While he shook in his doublet with fear.

The next that came up were four robbers,
Well-mounted on brave prancing nags,
She desired them to stand and deliver
And told them she wanted their bags.

The highwaymen all drew their rapiers,
She bid them stand on their guard,
Then away this fair maid did caper,
The highwaymen followed her hard.

They followed and soon overtook her,
And gathered so fiercely around,
But as they made search for the lucre
By Jakers! a woman they found.

Index